THE
CHARLES MANSON
MURDER TRIAL

A Headline Court Case

Headline Court Cases

The Aaron Burr Treason Trial
A Headline Court Case
0-7660-1765-6

The Chicago "Black Sox" Baseball Scandal
A Headline Court Case
0-7660-2044-4

The Chicago Seven Political Protest Trial
A Headline Court Case
0-7660-1764-8

The Court-Martial Trial of West Point Cadet Johnson Whittaker
A Headline Court Case
0-7660-1485-1

The Haymarket Square Riot Trial
A Headline Court Case
0-7660-1761-3

The Lizzie Borden "Axe Murder" Trial
A Headline Court Case
0-7660-1422-3

The Mary Surratt "Lincoln Assassination" Trial
A Headline Court Case
0-7660-1481-9

The "Mississippi Burning" Civil Rights Murder Conspiracy Trial
A Headline Court Case
0-7660-1762-1

The O. J. Simpson Murder Trial
A Headline Court Case
0-7660-1480-0

The Salem Witchcraft Trials
A Headline Court Case
0-7660-1383-9

The Scopes Monkey Trial
A Headline Court Case
0-7660-1388-X

The Susan B. Anthony Women's Voting Rights Trial
A Headline Court Case
0-7660-1759-1

The Teapot Dome Scandal Trial
A Headline Court Case
0-7660-1484-3

The Terrorist Trial of the 1993 Bombing of the World Trade Center
A Headline Court Case
0-7660-2045-2

The Trial of Gangster Al Capone
A Headline Court Case
0-7660-1482-7

Headline Court Cases

THE
CHARLES MANSON
MURDER TRIAL

A Headline Court Case

Michael J. Pellowski

Enslow Publishers, Inc.
40 Industrial Road   PO Box 38
Box 398   Aldershot
Berkeley Heights, NJ 07922   Hants GU12 6BP
USA   UK
http://www.enslow.com

To old friends . . . Harold Hahn and Mark Mazura

Copyright © 2004 by Michael J. Pellowski

All rights reserved.

No part of this book may be reproduced by any means
without the written permission of the publisher.

Library of Congress Cataloging-in-Publication Data

Pellowski, Michael J.
    The Charles Manson murder trial : a headline court case / Michael J. Pellowski.—
1st ed.
        v. cm. — (Headline court cases)
    Includes bibliographical references and index.
    Contents: Brutal murder & bloody messages — The crimes — The investigation —
A case of murder— Prosecution — The trial— The sentence & afterwards.
    ISBN 0-7660-2167-X
    1. Manson, Charles, 1934– —Trials, litigation, etc.—Juvenile literature. 2. Trials
(Murder)—California—Juvenile literature. 3. Mass murder—California—Juvenile
literature. [1. Manson, Charles, 1934– —Trials, litigation, etc. 2. Trials (Murder)
3. Mass murder.] I. Title. II. Series.
   KF224.M212P45 2004
   345.73'02523'09794—dc22
                        2003026607

Printed in the United States of America

10 9 8 7 6 5 4 3 2 1

Illustration Credits: All photos are from AP/Wide World.

Cover Illustration: AP/Wide World.

Contents

chapter one

BLOODY MESSAGES

BLOODY MURDER—A brutal killing spree in the summer of 1969 baffled police and terrified residents of California's wealthiest communities. There were a total of eight dead bodies at three murder scenes. Among those killed were a wealthy heiress from a famous family, a well-known Hollywood hairdresser, and a beautiful young actress who was eight months pregnant at the time of her death.

The crime of murder is always revolting, but these acts were savage beyond belief. Some of the victims were beaten and then stabbed. Others were shot and stabbed. Still others were tied up and then stabbed to death. One victim was found with a large serving fork stuck into his body.

Investigators struggled to come up with motives or suspects in the crimes. At first the Los Angeles Police Department (LAPD) did not think the murders were connected. The only vague link between the deaths of six men and two women were words printed by the murderers at the scenes. The words were written with the blood of the victims.

The scene of the first murder was a Malibu Beach house. In July 1969, Gary Hinman, a young music teacher, was attacked in his home. He was stabbed several times and left to die. After a few days, police discovered his lifeless body. They also found two words written in Hinman's blood on the wall near the corpse: "Political Piggy."

In August of that same year, news of a horrible mass murder appeared in newspaper headlines all across America. Three men and two women were shot and stabbed to death in a posh Beverly Hills, California, home. The crime occurred at a house owned by Rudi Altobelli. Altobelli worked in the entertainment business and was well known to Hollywood celebrities as an agent and manager. At the time, Altobelli's main house was rented to Hollywood film director Roman Polanski. Altobelli's caretaker, William Garretson, lived in a guest cottage to the rear of the main residence. Polanski was not at his rented home in August 1969. He was away working on a film project.

At the time of the murders, Sharon Tate, an actress who was Polanski's wife, was staying at the house. Tate was eight months pregnant and was eagerly awaiting the birth of her first child. Visiting Sharon Tate that evening were several family friends. One was Abigail Folger, a wealthy coffee heiress. Another guest was Jay Sebring, a well-known Hollywood hairdresser, who was a frequent companion of Sharon Tate. The final member of the group that night was

The body of actress Sharon Tate is removed from the house on Cielo Drive. The brutal slaying of Tate, three of her friends, and an acquaintance of the caretaker baffled investigators and horrified the country.

Voytek Frykowski, Folger's lover and a close friend of Roman Polanski.

Visiting with caretaker William Garretson was a young man named Steve Parent. Parent was just leaving the Altobelli property when the killers arrived. He was in the wrong place at the wrong time and a victim of deadly circumstance.

Once again, the killers left behind a bizarre message. Sharon Tate's blood had been used to scribble a one-word message on a door: "Pig."

The next day, the killing spree continued. This time the murder scene was the Los Feliz district of Los Angeles. The victims were a married couple named Leno and Rosemary LaBianca. Leno LaBianca was a wealthy, middle-aged businessman. He was the president of a successful chain of supermarkets in the LA area. The LaBiancas were murdered after returning home from a boating trip to Lake Isabella, a popular California resort area.

Once again, the slayings were excessively brutal. Leno LaBianca was killed in his living room. A lamp cord was knotted around his neck. His hands were tied behind his back with a leather strap. He had been stabbed many times. Stuck in his abdomen were a knife and a large, ivory-handled serving fork. Carved into the flesh of his stomach was the word "War."

Rosemary LaBianca was murdered in her bedroom. A pillowcase was pulled over her head and a lamp cord was wrapped around her throat. She had been stabbed over and over again. The bed she lay in was soaked with her blood.

Again, the killers left messages using the blood of the victims. On one wall was scribbled "Death to Pigs." On another wall was printed the word "Rise." And written on the refrigerator door in the LaBiancas' kitchen were two strange words: "Healter Skelter."

At first, no one knew what the words meant or where they originated. Finally, it was realized that "healter skelter" was a misspelling of the song title "Helter Skelter," which had been recorded by the world-famous rock group the Beatles. The meaning of the phrase remained a mystery.

The police only had one clue that might link the three crimes together. Variations of the word "pig" were left at all of the murder scenes. Was it a coincidence or a connection? Detectives disagreed on that point.

Detective K. J. McCauley of the LAPD gave a statement to reporters after the LaBianca murders. "I don't see any connection between this murder and the others," said the detective. "They're too widely removed. I just don't see any connection."[1]

Bryce Houchin, a Los Angeles police sergeant, was not as certain as McCauley. He thought there might be a connection between the three cases. "There is a similarity," Sergeant Houchin told reporters, "but whether it's the same suspect or a copycat we just don't know."[2]

One of the problems with the theory that the three cases were related was that a suspect in the Gary Hinman murder case was Robert "Bobby" Beausoleil. He was in custody of the Los Angeles Sheriff's Office at the time of the other murders. Beausoleil had been arrested while driving Gary Hinman's car, which was missing from Hinman's home.

Bobby Beausoleil and Gary Hinman were casual friends. Beausoleil claimed that Hinman had loaned him the car. However, evidence suggested otherwise. Sheriff's officers found a knife hidden in the tire well of the vehicle. Beausoleil's pants were stained with blood.

Bobby Beausoleil was a handsome young musician who resented authority figures and did not like rules. He believed in free love, experimental drug use, and an easy lifestyle that did not include working for a living.

Beausoleil was also a member of a strange group living in the California desert. The group was a type of cult. A cult

A member of the family of Leno and Rosemary LaBianca holds up a photo of the couple at a court hearing. At the LaBianca murder scene was the first appearance of the odd phrase "Helter Skelter."

is a group of individuals fanatically devoted to a leader, concept, or idea. Cults often utilize strange rituals and despise people opposed to their beliefs. As a member of a potentially violent cult, Beausoleil was likely to be involved in criminal activities. He was a solid suspect in the Hinman crime.

However, police wondered, if Bobby Beausoleil was in police custody at the time of the Tate-LaBianca murders (as they were called by the press), how could the three crimes be connected? Many LAPD detectives believed the Tate murders were in some way associated with a drug deal. (The police knew that hairdresser Jay Sebring had used drugs and had acquaintances who were drug dealers.) However, police did not believe that drugs had anything to do with the LaBianca murders. They believed the motive in that crime might be robbery. A few minor items were missing from the LaBianca home, including Rosemary LaBianca's wallet and wristwatch.

Another problem that plagued the investigation from the outset was jurisdiction. Because of where the crimes were committed, different police agencies were involved as the prime investigators. The Tate and LaBianca murders were under the jurisdiction of the LAPD. The Hinman murder case was under the jurisdiction of the Los Angeles Sheriff's Office (LASO). At first, each department conducted its own separate investigation without pooling resources or data.

Nevertheless, investigators from the LASO felt the three crimes were connected, mainly because of the bloody messages at the scenes. But the LAPD investigators saw no logical link between the homicides. The position of the LASO made no sense to the LAPD. The Los Angeles Police Department considered the words written in blood a coincidence.

Officials of the LAPD did not know they were dealing with a complex, criminal mastermind and cult leader who had a bizarre plan. The name of Charles Manson had not yet surfaced in the investigation. Investigators did not realize that Manson was the leader of the hippie cult Bobby Beausoleil belonged to. They did not know anything about Charles Manson. They did not know how Charles Manson's mind worked.

"No sense makes sense," Charles Manson had once said.[3] Manson's plan included senseless murders. His plan was called Helter Skelter.

chapter two

THE CULT AND THE CRIMES

MANSON FAMILY—The cult group Bobby Beausoleil belonged to was known as "the Family" by its followers. The head of the Family and the leader of the cult was Charles Manson. Manson was born on November 12, 1934, in Cincinnati, Ohio. His mother was a young prostitute who frequently drank. Her name was Kathleen Maddox. She was just sixteen years old and unmarried when her son, Charles, was born.

Kathleen Maddox married a boyfriend named Bill Manson a short time after the birth of her son. Charles took the last name of Manson, even though Manson was not his birth father. The name of Charles Manson's real father is still a mystery.

When Charles was only five years old, his mother got into trouble with the police. Kathleen Maddox was arrested for armed robbery and sent to jail for five years. Young Charles Manson went to live with his maternal grandmother. Charles' grandmother was obsessively religious. She taught young Charles the virtues of Christian meekness. Charles became a quiet and timid youngster. When Charles Manson could no longer live with his grandmother for economic reasons, he was sent to live with an uncle and aunt in McMechen, West Virginia.

The uncle of Charles Manson felt his nephew's timidity was unmanly. He wanted the boy to be tough. He sent Charles to school dressed as a girl. The purpose was to humiliate the boy so he would fight anyone who dared to insult him.[1] Charles Manson quickly learned how to fight. He toughened up and forgot all about the Christian virtue of being meek.

In 1942, Kathleen Maddox was paroled and reclaimed her son. Charles Manson was eight years old at the time. Mother and son spent the next several years living in cheap hotel rooms with various men. In 1947, Kathleen Maddox tried to have her son placed in a foster home. None were available. Twelve-year-old Charles Manson was taken away from his mother by the court and sent to the Gibault School for Boys in Terre Haute, Indiana. Ten months later, Charles Manson ran away from the school. He stayed on the run and turned to crime in order to survive. Young Charles Manson committed a series of crimes. He was caught during one of many burglaries and sent to a juvenile center in Indianapolis, Indiana. He escaped and was recaptured. He was sent to Father Flanagan's Boys Town, but ran away shortly after his arrival and continued his life of crime. At age thirteen, Charles Manson committed his first armed robbery. He was arrested and sent to the Indiana School for Boys.

In 1951, at the age of sixteen, Charles Manson escaped from the Indiana School for Boys and continued to support himself by robbing and stealing. He stole a car and drove it over a state boundary. Driving a stolen car over a state line is a federal crime and a very serious offense. He was captured outside of Beaver, Utah, and sent to the National Training School for Boys in Washington, D.C. While there, Manson developed an interest in music. It was one of the two subjects Manson liked. The other was auto mechanics. In 1954, Charles Manson was paroled. He was nineteen years old at the time.

After his release Charles Manson met a young waitress named Rosalie Jean Willis. The two young people began a relationship. In January 1955, Charles Manson married Rosalie Jean Willis. To support his new wife, Manson worked as a busboy and gas station attendant—and also stole cars.

Once again, Charles Manson was arrested. He was captured in California and charged with driving a stolen car across state lines. With him at the time was his pregnant wife, Rosalie. At first, Manson was given probation by a judge who felt sorry for the father-to-be. Manson quickly broke his probation and was sent to Terminal Island Reformatory in San Pedro, California. He was in jail when his wife Rosalie gave birth to Charles Manson, Jr. Manson attempted to escape. Five years were added to his sentence. In 1958, Rosalie divorced him. Charles Manson, Sr., had no further contact with his wife or son from that day on. He would later build a new family for himself.

Charles Manson, shown here in 1970, was arrested many times and spent much of his life in jail and other correctional institutions.

Manson spent the next several years of his life in and out of jail. In 1967, he was again locked up in Terminal Island Reformatory in California. This time he was in jail for forging a treasury check. When the date of his release came, Manson begged the prison officials to let him stay, because prison life was the only life he knew. Manson had spent most of his young adult life in various institutions. He was not sure he could cope with living out in the real world. Nevertheless, Charles Manson was set free.

The Hippies

The year was 1967. It was a time of radical changes in America. Young people across the country were rebelling against authority. Many dropped out of society. They claimed to be protesting the American culture of materialism, racism, and political corruption; they also opposed the war in Vietnam. Many looked for a revolution, either peaceful or violent, that would change the world. Many were opposed to the power structure, which they referred to as "the Establishment" or "the pigs." Many of them also believed in sexual experimentation and in the use of mind-altering drugs like LSD and marijuana. They were called hippies, flower children, and "the Counterculture."

Charles Manson headed for the Haight-Ashbury section of San Francisco, California. Haight-Ashbury was a center for hippies and young people interested in art, poetry, and music. Manson had hopes of pursuing a career in music. He had been inspired by the songs of the Beatles, a British rock 'n' roll group that had taken the world by storm. Charles Manson wanted to make music like the Beatles. He believed their songs had very important words of wisdom for young people to live by. Manson thought there were secret messages in the lyrics of some Beatles songs.

The Manson Family

In 1969, after the Hinman and Tate-LaBianca murders, the police conducted a raid on a ranch in the desert where the Manson Family resided. The purpose of the raid was to break up a stolen car ring operating at that site. Netted in the

The Haight-Ashbury district in San Francisco was a magnet for hippies and other unconventional youth during the 1960s.

police raid was Susan Atkins, a devout follower of Charles Manson. While in custody, Atkins, who was also called Sadie Mae Glutz by Family members, was implicated in the Gary Hinman murder. Family member Kitty Lutesinger, who had been Bobby Beausoleil's girlfriend, told police about Atkins's involvement in the case.

While in jail, Susan Atkins did not try to conceal the role she played in the gruesome crime. In fact, she boasted to cell mates about her involvement in several murder schemes.

"We wanted to do a crime that would shock the world, that the world would have to stand up and take notice," Atkins told her cell mates.[2] Susan Atkins was typical of the type of individuals who flocked to the Family of Charles Manson. She was young, rebellious, and a little deranged. Susan Atkins felt no remorse about killing people. It was all part of her leader's master plan.

Who were the disciples of Charles Manson? How did he assemble a tightly knit group of misfits who were willing to kill on his command?

The Manson Family began in 1967 on a sidewalk in Venice, California. A seventeen-year-old woman was sitting on the curb. She had scraggly red hair, was dressed like a hippie, and was crying. Her name was Lynette Fromme, and she had no place to go. Her parents had thrown her out. Up walked Charles Manson. Fromme later described their first encounter:

> A man walked up and said, your father kicked you out of the house. He asked me to come with him. I said no . . . and he said he'd like me to come, but could not make up my mind

for me. No one had ever treated me like that—he did not push me—so I picked up all that I had and went with him. That was Charles Manson.

Fromme later added, "A dog goes to somebody who loves it and takes care of it."[3]

Lynette Fromme—whom Manson nicknamed "Squeaky"—became one of Manson's first followers, along with fellow hippie Mary Brunner. Charles Manson took on the role of spiritual leader. He spouted twisted biblical philosophy and made connections between religion and rock 'n' roll music. His followers thought of him as a prophet or savior. Manson frequented the streets of California cities looking for homeless runaways to join his band. Among his recruits was Bobby Beausoleil. Beausoleil's rugged good looks and reputation as a musician helped attract young women to Manson's Family. Once part of the group, the young followers enjoyed listening to Charles Manson talk about his predictions for society and the world. He foretold of a country stripped bare of hated laws and regulations, a world ruled by young hippies. Slowly, Manson's following grew into a cult of fifty or more people. All were people who had difficulty fitting into normal society. They found Manson's words hypnotic. To them, Charles Manson was a god.

In addition to his devout cult members, Charles Manson also had friends who were frequent visitors to the Family's headquarters in the desert. Those visitors enjoyed the company of the young women, most of whom believed in free love. They also visited the ranch to drink and experiment with drugs. Those visitors included aspiring Western actor Donald Shea (nicknamed Shorty), music teacher Gary Hinman, and motorcycle gang members Danny DeCarlo and Al Springer.

At first the Manson Family lived in an old school bus

Major Manson Family Members
(nicknames in parentheses)

Charles Manson, head of the Family

Susan Denise Atkins (Sadie Mae Glutz)

Bobby Beausoleil

Mary Brunner

Bruce Davis

Juan Flynn

Lynnette Fromme (Squeaky)

Steve Grogan (Clem Tufts)

Barbara Hoyt

Linda Kasabian

Patricia Krenwinkel (Katie)

Dianne Lake (Snake)

Kitty Lutesinger

Ruth Ann Moorehouse (Ouisch)

Catherine Share (Gypsy)

Leslie Van Houten (LuLu; Leslie Sankston)

Paul Alan Watkins

Charles Watson (Tex)

that they drove from place to place in the desert. The Family survived by begging for money from strangers and stealing. Stealing cars—especially Volkswagens—was a favorite way for the Family to get cash.

After spending a year moving from place to place, the Manson Family found a permanent home. Squeaky Fromme discovered the perfect place: an empty group of buildings known as the Spahn Movie Ranch. The ranch was owned by a nearly blind semi-invalid named George Spahn. Spahn seldom visited the isolated site in the desert. He lived elsewhere. The ranch had been used for the filming of movie Westerns many years earlier. It was located way out in the desert near the Santa Susana Mountains on the outskirts of Los Angeles.

Charles Manson went to George Spahn and asked for permission to camp at the abandoned movie site. Since many of Manson's female followers were kind and helpful to Spahn, assisting him in performing everyday chores, he agreed. The Manson Family moved into the Spahn Movie Ranch. George Spahn did not know what kind of people he was dealing with. He believed the group was a harmless band of hippies looking to escape the problems of modern society. Of course, he was very wrong.

Having a permanent home base helped Manson's family of runaways and misfits to grow. Charles Manson soon found another nearby ranch to use as living quarters for his new followers. It was a ranch owned by Arlene Barker. Like George Spahn, Arlene Barker did not live at her ranch in the desert. Once again, Charles Manson asked for and received permission to camp at the site. Members of the Manson Family moved into the Barker Ranch. Slowly but surely, Charles Manson was establishing a strange colony of faithful followers out in the remote California desert. The Barker Ranch was located in an almost inaccessible area south of Death Valley National Monument. It guaranteed the Family privacy and a degree of safety. It was also the perfect place for Charles Manson to indoctrinate his followers into his bizarre philosophy of life.

Charles Manson believed that man is not separate from nature. He felt mankind was closely tied to nature's laws— the law of the jungle, the survival of the fittest. He wanted his Family to live according to the laws of nature, not according to the laws of men. He thought killing and death were part of nature's laws. According to Manson, it was all right to eliminate people for a purpose. He believed that murder was not a crime; it was a natural act.

"Humans are pretty stupid," Manson said. "Humans won't survive."[4] Manson was talking about certain members of society whom he considered human cattle. They were useless and unimportant in the future Manson predicted.

"I don't think in goods or bads, just is's, what *it* is. Not what I was, want or hope. Whatever life is, it is, and bad and good got nothing to do with it. A snake eats the baby squirrel. Mama squirrel may say that's bad, but snakes got to eat," Manson said.[5]

Charles Manson did not care about the laws of society. He did not think such laws applied to him or his followers. The Manson Family rejected society and its morals. Manson planned to create an entirely new world that he and his followers would rule.

The Helter Skelter Plan

Charles Manson believed that the lyrics of certain Beatles songs contained secret messages. Manson thought he was a prophet who could decipher the messages. He often compared the lyrics to passages in the Bible, especially chapters in the Book of Revelation. For instance, one verse states: "There came out of the smoke locusts upon the earth; and unto them was given power" (Chapter 9, verse 3). Manson claimed the locusts were actually the Beatles. Elsewhere it said, "Their faces were as the faces of men, [yet] they had hair as the hair of women." (Chapter 9, verses 7–8). The Beatles were one of the first male groups to wear their hair long.[6]

Manson convinced his followers that the Bible prophesied the coming of the Beatles and that concealed in the group's songs were holy messages calling for action. Charles Manson analyzed the lyrics of the Beatles song "Blackbird." He told his followers that "Blackbird" was about the civil rights struggle of African Americans in the United States. He claimed that the lyric "Blackbird . . . arise" was a call for a race war in America.

According to Manson, the war would be savage and bloody. It would cause total confusion in the world. Members of the black and white races would slaughter each other, killing indiscriminately. The Manson Family would weather the racial storm by hiding in the desert until the

The Beatles, a British rock 'n' roll group, were world-famous. Charles Manson thought that the lyrics of their popular songs contained secret messages for him.

killing ceased. Manson called the global race conflict "Helter Skelter." He took the term "Helter Skelter" from another Beatles song. Manson thought the words were a divine message. He did not know they were really about an amusement park ride.

Manson predicted that Helter Skelter would begin with a series of atrocious murders. He told his Family that African Americans from Watts, a minority neighborhood in Los Angeles, would cut up rich white people and smear the blood of their victims on doors and walls. Angry white people would then strike back by going into Watts and slaughtering African Americans. Some members of the white race would then side with their African-American friends. Battle lines would be drawn setting brother against brother. Soon the entire world would be in racial turmoil. The only white people to survive the holocaust would be the Manson Family. Remaining survivors of the black race would then look to Charles Manson and his followers for leadership and guidance.[7] Manson believed that he would then seize control of the world and rule the earth.

Charles Manson was eager to assume the position of power he thought he would inherit. Instead of waiting for Helter Skelter to begin on its own, Manson decided to start the ball rolling himself. He would orchestrate the first brutal killings that would incite the race war.

The Hinman Murder

Gary Hinman was a music teacher, and Manson and some of his followers were musicians (or considered themselves to be). Hinman had been loosely associated with the Manson Family. He had visited the Spahn Movie Ranch. Hinman was killed by members of the Manson Family in the summer of 1969. His death had nothing to do with the Helter Skelter plans of Charles Manson.

When Manson heard a rumor that Hinman had inherited some money, he sent a group of his followers to Hinman's beach cottage in Malibu. Charles Manson wanted that money.

Manson Family members Bobby Beausoleil, Susan Atkins, and Mary Brunner went to Gary Hinman's house to get the money on July 25, 1969. After some general chitchat, Beausoleil demanded that Hinman turn over the money. He told Hinman that Manson wanted it. Hinman flatly refused to give Beausoleil any money. Bobby Beausoleil began to beat Gary Hinman, then pulled out a hunting knife and slashed Hinman's face. Hinman ended up dazed and cut from the savage beating he received from Beausoleil.

While the women held the semiconscious man hostage, Bobby Beausoleil contacted Charles Manson, who was waiting at the Spahn Ranch. Beausoleil told Manson that Gary Hinman refused to turn over the money. Manson decided to deal with Hinman himself. He traveled to Hinman's home, bringing with him a sharp sword he kept at the Spahn Ranch.

When Manson arrived, Hinman was partially recovered. There was another scuffle, during which Manson hacked off a piece of Gary Hinman's ear with the sword. Then Bobby Beausoleil, with the help of Susan Atkins, stabbed Hinman numerous times with a hunting knife. As Hinman lay sprawled on the floor, Beausoleil dipped his hand in Hinman's blood. He then made a bloody handprint on the wall to plant a false clue. Beausoleil hoped the police would mistakenly connect the clue to the Black Panthers, a militant African-American group that advocated violence against white society in their attempt to secure equal rights for black people.

Susan Atkins then used Hinman's blood to write the words "Political Piggy" on the wall near the body. Next, the Family members stole Gary Hinman's Volkswagen bus and his Fiat station wagon. They drove the vehicles back to the ranch in the desert.

Gary Hinman lay on the floor bleeding and unconscious until he died from his wounds two days later. On July 31, officers from the Los Angeles Sheriff's Office went to Hinman's house to check on the thirty-four-year-old music teacher who had mysteriously dropped out of sight, and they discovered the body.

On August 6, Bobby Beausoleil was stopped by officers of the LASO while driving Hinman's missing Fiat. Beausoleil's clothes had dried blood on them. The knife used to kill Hinman was found hidden in the car. Beausoleil was immediately taken into custody.

The Tate Murders

Charles Manson was a well-spoken individual who impressed and interested a lot of people. For a time, he pursued a career in music and met some important show business people in California. He became acquainted with

Dennis Wilson, a member of the Beach Boys, a famous group. He also knew talent scout Gregg Jakobson, who was married to the daughter of well-known comedian Lou Costello (of Abbott and Costello). Jakobson introduced Manson to Terry Melcher, the son of singer and movie star Doris Day. Melcher was also in the record business. Jakobson thought Melcher might want to record Manson. After hearing Charles Manson's music, Melcher declined.

Terry Melcher lived at 10050 Cielo Drive, in a secluded area of Beverly Hills. He later sold that house to Rudi Altobelli. Altobelli, who traveled a great deal, rented the

In his attempts to start a musical career, Manson met Dennis Wilson, a member of the Beach Boys. (Wilson is at the bottom center of this 1966 photo.)

home out to film director Roman Polanski and his actress wife Sharon Tate.

After being initially turned down by Terry Melcher, Charles Manson let some time pass. Manson then went to Melcher's former home, hoping to persuade Melcher to reconsider his position. Instead of Terry Melcher, Charles Manson found new residents at the house. Rudi Altobelli and his friends were not interested in dealing with Charles Manson. He was treated rudely and turned away from the door.

When Manson decided to kick-start Helter Skelter, that isolated house came to his mind. Why? No one knows for sure. Whatever the reason, Manson sent Family members Charles "Tex" Watson, Susan Atkins, Patricia Krenwinkel, and Linda Kasabian to 10050 Cielo Drive on August 8, 1969. It was the night the madness of Helter Skelter began.

Manson told the women to get an extra change of clothes, a driver's license, and knives. Tex Watson carried a nine-shot .22 caliber Hi Standard Longhorn revolver. This type of revolver has a very long barrel; it is commonly referred to as a Buntline Special, because the model was originally ordered by Western pulp writer Ned Buntline for Marshall Wyatt Earp. The four Family members left the Spahn Ranch in an old Ford. In the back of the Ford were a pair of wire cutters and a length of nylon rope.

Tex Watson was familiar with the house at 10050 Cielo Drive. However, he did not know who lived in the house. Manson and his Family did not know or care if Rudi

Altobelli still lived there. Who lived there really did not matter to the plan.

Watson parked the car a short distance from the main gate to the house, which was closed and locked. The women carried their extra clothing, which was tied in bundles, and their knives. The group avoided using the gate. They thought it might have an alarm system. Instead, they climbed over a short fence that encircled the property.

Once inside the wall, the Family members snipped the telephone wires. They were then surprised by a car approaching the front gate. It was a Rambler. Its headlights flashed in front of their eyes. Driving the car was eighteen-year-old Steve Parent. Parent was departing after visiting his friend, nineteen-year-old William Garretson, who was the caretaker. Garretson lived in a guest cottage separate from the main house.

Tex Watson told the women to hide. He then stepped into the path of the car and flagged it down. The Rambler stopped. Watson approached the driver, gun in hand. He fired one shot and then three more, killing Steve Parent. Watson turned off the car's motor and lights. The women joined Watson and together they pushed the car containing Parent's body off to the side.

When the group reached the house, Watson, Atkins, and Krenwinkel went inside. Kasabian remained outside as a lookout.

About a mile away, a man named Tim Ireland was supervising a children's campout. He heard a scream that chilled him: "Oh God, no, please don't!"[8]

Neighbors of the Tates heard gunshots. Neighborhood dogs began to bark. A private security patrol officer named Robert Bullington heard shots and alerted Eric Karlson, who was working at security headquarters. Karlson called the LAPD to report the shots. The police department also had a report of a woman screaming in the area. Police response to the sound of shots and screams was slow in coming. Amazingly, caretaker William Garretson was busy in his cottage and did not hear the ruckus.

Meanwhile, inside the Tate house, the Manson Family members were beginning Helter Skelter. Watson had entered the house through a window and opened a door for the women. They found Voytek Frykowski dozing on the couch in the living room. He woke up and asked who the intruders were.

"I am the Devil and I'm here to do the Devil's business," Tex Watson replied.[9] He waved a gun at Frykowski and ordered him to keep still. Watson then sent Susan Atkins to search the house for other inhabitants. Atkins found Abigail Folger in a bedroom reading. She also found Jay Sebring and Sharon Tate in another room talking. Voytek Frykowski was tied up with the rope they had brought, and the others were ushered into the living room. When Jay Sebring protested, Tex Watson hit him with the gun and then shot him. Sharon Tate and Abigail Folger screamed. Watson ordered them to be quiet, and they obeyed. Watson placed a rope around the necks of Sebring, Tate, and Folger and told Susan Atkins, who was armed with a knife, to kill Frykowski. Frykowski began to fight. Atkins stabbed and

Tex Watson, a member of Manson's bizarre Family, took part in the brutal murders of August 1969. "I am the Devil and I'm here to do the Devil's business," he announced to his victims at the Tate home.

slashed him. The wounded man made a dash for the front door in an attempt to escape. Watson ran after Frykowski and hit him on the head with the butt of the gun. The gun's handle grips broke and pieces went flying. After that, the gun would not work. Watson was also armed with a knife. Watson and Atkins stabbed Frykowski.

Abigail Folger freed herself from the rope and began to fight with Patricia Krenwinkel in a desperate attempt to flee the scene. Krenwinkel and Watson stabbed Folger. Her body ended up out on the lawn by the front door near Frykowski's body.

Susan Atkins guarded Sharon Tate. When Tex Watson returned, he told Atkins to kill her. Sharon Tate begged for her life. She pleaded for her unborn child, to no avail. Susan Atkins and Tex Watson ruthlessly stabbed the pregnant woman.

The killers then exited the scene of their grisly crime. Watson halted outside and told Susan Atkins to go back inside the house. He ordered her to write a message in blood on the door of the house. Atkins returned to the body of Sharon Tate. She picked up a towel and dipped it into Tate's blood. Then she took the blood-soaked towel and wrote the word "pig" on the front door. She threw the towel down; it landed on Jay Sebring's lifeless face.

Linda Kasabian was not directly outside of the house; she was on the other side of the wall, waiting by the parked car. Atkins, Krenwinkel, and Watson were soaked in blood. They picked up their extra clothing. Tex Watson pushed the button that opened the front gate, leaving a bloody print on the button. They walked out, accidentally leaving behind one of the knives used in the murder.

In the car, the three changed out of their bloody clothes. On the way back to the ranch, the killers disposed of their bloody clothes and their weapons. They pulled over on an embankment and tossed them off a cliff. Then they drove to the Spahn Ranch to report back to Charles Manson.

The victims left behind had been brutally butchered. In all, the four victims inside the house received over one

Black Panthers Bobby Seale and Huey Newton pose in front of party headquarters. Manson and the Family hoped that their murder spree would be blamed on militant African Americans.

hundred stab wounds. Abigail Folger had been stabbed twenty-eight times. Voytek Frykowski had been shot twice, struck over the head with a blunt object thirteen times, and stabbed fifty-one times. Jay Sebring had been shot once, hit, and stabbed seven times. Sharon Tate had been stabbed sixteen times.

The LaBianca Murders

When Watson and the women reported back to Charles Manson after murdering Tate and her friends, he was upset. He was not pleased with the way the job had been carried out. He thought the murders were too messy. The next time, Manson said, the crime would be more organized. The next time came on the very next night, August 9.

Once again, Charles Manson told Susan Atkins and the others to collect extra clothing. Tex Watson, Patricia Krenwinkel, and Linda Kasabian all obeyed their leader's orders. This time Charles Manson himself decided to lead the group, which now included Steve ("Clem") Grogan and Leslie Van Houten. The group got into the old Ford and drove around looking for a place to commit random murder. They stopped at one place to check out a potential site. Manson looked through a window and saw photographs of children on a wall. Because of that, Manson decided to select another house.

The house eventually chosen by the Manson Family belonged to Leno and Rosemary LaBianca. Their home was next to a house where Charles Manson and some members of the Family had gone to a drug party a year earlier.

Manson went into the house first. He came out with a woman's wallet. Manson then ordered Tex Watson, Patricia Krenwinkel, and Leslie Van Houten to kill the people inside. He also told them to hitchhike back to the ranch. Manson, Atkins, Grogan, and Kasabian then drove off.

Leno LaBianca was in the living room reading the Sunday morning papers when the killers entered his home. Watson confronted LaBianca, while Krenwinkel and Van Houten took Rosemary LaBianca into the bedroom. Tex Watson stabbed Leno LaBianca, who began to scream. Rosemary LaBianca struggled with her captors. Leslie Van Houten held down Mrs. LaBianca as Patricia Krenwinkel took a fork out of the LaBianca kitchen and stuck it into Leno LaBianca's stomach. She also carved the word "War" into his abdomen with a knife. Then they wrote in blood "Death to All Pigs" and "Rise" on the walls and "Healter Skelter" on the refrigerator door.

On the drive back to the ranch, Charles Manson stopped at a gas station in an African-American neighborhood. He left the wallet he had taken from the LaBianca residence in the gas station bathroom. Manson hoped a black person would find the wallet and use the credit cards inside. He wanted the use of stolen credit cards to be traced back to a person of color. If that happened, he thought, it would hasten the progress of Helter Skelter.

chapter three

THE INVESTIGATION

THE CRIME SCENE—Winifred Chapman, Sharon Tate's housekeeper, arrived at the home of Tate and Roman Polanski a little after 8:00 A.M. on August 9, 1969. She saw a fallen telephone wire hanging over the main gate. The sight puzzled her, but did not worry her. She activated the main gate's mechanism, and the gate swung open. The housekeeper walked into the estate and noticed an unfamiliar white Rambler parked in the driveway at an odd angle. The strange car did not alarm her. She was accustomed to seeing unfamiliar cars parked at the residence in the early hours of the morning. The Polanskis often had parties that lasted very late. Guests—many of them Hollywood celebrities—frequently stayed the night.

Chapman walked toward the house. The outside lights were still on. That struck her as odd. The housekeeper shut the lights off. Using a key left in a secret place near a side entrance, she unlocked the door and went into the Polanski house. Chapman went through a hall and walked toward the dining room. She stopped. Two large steamer trunks blocked her path. They had not been there the day before. Blood appeared to be on the trunks. She also saw two bloody towels. Chapman crept forward cautiously, sensing that something was wrong. She saw more splashes of blood. Through the open door of another entranceway leading outside, Chapman spied a body lying in a heap on the lawn. She ran screaming from the house and fled toward the front gate. She passed the white Rambler again. This time she peered inside the car. Chapman saw a dead body inside the car. She raced to the house next door and frantically pounded on the front door.

"Murder, death, bodies, blood!" Winifred Chapman shrieked as she pounded.[1] When no one answered, she ran to the next house, which was owned by the Asin family. They let her in and phoned police.

The first Los Angeles Police Department officer to arrive at the scene was Jerry DeRosa. He was in a car on a one-man patrol. Officer DeRosa began to question the hysterical housekeeper. The woman was so upset that the policeman could not make sense of her answers. It was neighbor Ray Asin who told DeRosa exactly who lived in the house where Chapman worked. Asin explained that the home belonged to Rudi Altobelli but was rented to movie director Roman Polanski and his wife, actress Sharon Tate. He told the officer that Polanski was away making a movie and that Abigail Folger and Voytek Frykowski were staying with Sharon Tate until her husband returned home. Asin also told DeRosa that a caretaker named William Garretson lived at the Altobelli home. When Mrs. Chapman finally calmed down, she added that Jay Sebring was at the Tate house. The housekeeper had noticed his car, a black Porsche, parked in the driveway.

Officer DeRosa got a rifle out of his patrol car. Then he had Mrs. Chapman show him how to open the front gate. He discovered the body in the Rambler. He did not know who the victim in the car was. At that time, a second police officer, William T. Whisenhunt, arrived. He armed himself with a shotgun, and the two policemen started toward the main house. They did not get far before they spotted two lifeless forms lying on the lawn near the house. At that time, a third policeman, Officer Robert Burbridge, joined DeRosa and Whisenhunt.

The three policemen reached the house but did not enter through the door. They did not know if the killer or killers were still inside. The men would be easy targets if they just walked in. DeRosa waited on the lawn while Whisenhunt and Burbridge climbed in a side window. They found the bodies of Jay Sebring and Sharon Tate and the bloody message inside.

The two officers were shocked and sickened by the murder scene. They composed themselves and began to search for the killer. As they left the main house and moved toward the guest house, a dog barked. Then the policemen heard the voice of someone trying to silence the dog.

The armed policemen jumped out and confronted young William Garretson. With Garretson was a dog owned by Rudi Altobelli. The officers subdued the dog and took the startled youth into custody. Garretson was shocked by the unexpected

This is the estate in Los Angeles that Sharon Tate and her husband, Roman Polanski, were renting from Rudi Altobelli. It was the scene of the grisly multiple murders.

turn of events. He claimed he had been busy writing letters while the murders were committed and had heard absolutely nothing. DeRosa read Garretson his rights and began taking him to the patrol car. The automatic front gate was closed. Officer DeRosa reached for the inside button that opened the gate. A bloody fingerprint left by killer Tex Watson was on the button. Officer DeRosa, without thinking, pressed the button and smeared the killer's fingerprint.

Clues and Evidence Mishandled

William Garretson was taken to police headquarters for questioning. At the same time, officers of the LAPD began their investigation at the murder scene. Officer Joe Granado, a forensic chemist with the Scientific Investigation Division (SID) went to work. His job was to find and save biological evidence such as strands of hair, blood, etc. More and more investigators kept arriving at the scene. Four detectives took charge of the initial investigations: Lieutenant R. C. Madlock, Lieutenant J. J. Gregoire, Sergeant F. Gravante, and Sergeant T. L. Rogers.

News of the murders leaked to the press. Sharon Tate, Roman Polanski, Abigail Folger, and Jay Sebring were well-known people. Reporters and news crews began to flock to the crime scene. Securing the site was difficult, if not impossible. The crime scene was crowded and somewhat disorganized. Clues were handled carelessly and disturbed.

Originally, two broken pistol grips (from the handle of the gun) were seen at an entrance hall near a door. Those same grips were later discovered under a chair in the living room. A third piece of the grip was found outside. (It was later deduced that they had been accidentally stepped on and kicked around.) Officers had also inadvertently tracked blood outside the house.

In addition to trampling evidence, the LAPD officers made other mistakes that could later damage a prosecutor's case. Police took sheets out of a linen closet and covered the bodies out on the lawn, which had been identified as Abigail Folger and Voytek Frykowski. (At first, Frykowski was thought to be Roman Polanski or a relative of Polanski.)

Officer Joe Granado took blood samples from the murder scene. The samples would be used to determine if the blood was human or animal. In 1969, blood testing was not as advanced as it is today. Sophisticated DNA tests were not available back then. The police wanted to know which blood came from which victim or possibly from the killer(s). If human, the blood type (A, B, AB, or O) and subtype would be determined. However, if the blood was dried, determining the exact subtype would be more difficult. It was a hot day and many of the blood samples were dry. Granado also made the mistake of overlooking some spots of blood. He took a total of forty-five blood samples, but determined the subtypes for only twenty-four of them. There was so much blood and blood evidence at the scene that Officer Granado was overwhelmed. However, he did turn up an important clue. He discovered a Buck brand pocketknife wedged in a cushion of a chair near Sharon Tate's body. The knife was believed to have been left behind by the killers. Another important clue was the rope that tied together the bodies of Tate and Sebring.

Other specialists worked the crime scene searching for fingerprints. Officers Jerrome A. Boen and D. L. Girt of the SID's latent print section spent over six hours collecting evidence.

The robbery homicide division of the LAPD took charge of the investigation. Sergeants Michael J. McGann and Jess Buckles were assigned to handle the case.

While the investigation got under way, movie director Roman Polanski was contacted on the set of the movie he was making in Europe. He was told that his wife and unborn child were victims of a horrible crime. The shaken director quickly made arrangements to return to the United States. Relatives of the other victims were also notified. Only one victim was still unknown to police. The young man found in the Rambler was considered a "John Doe" (a name for a person whose identity is unknown). The police did not know who the man in the car was during the early stages of the investigation. Because of shoddy police work, they had not yet come up with the name of the victim who had been gunned down in the driveway.

Strange Motives

The press had a field day proposing possible motives for the horrible mass murder. The towel thrown on Jay Sebring's head was mistakenly reported to be a white hood. Newspaper reports strained to make a connection between the towel and the Ku Klux Klan, a racist terrorist group whose members dressed in white hoods. Other newspapers suggested the crime was the ritual work of a devil-worship cult. Other reports suggested the murders were the work of Mafia hit men or foreign secret service agents.

The LAPD had a different theory. It was the opinion of the police that the crime had something to do with drugs. Jay Sebring had been known to use drugs. Small amounts of cocaine and marijuana were discovered in his Porsche at the residence. A bag of marijuana was found in a cabinet in the living room inside the house. At an earlier party thrown by Roman Polanski and Sharon Tate, two well-known drug dealers had been in attendance. The dealers had started an argument and been removed from the party on Polanski's orders. The disturbance was noted in a police report of the incident. The police wondered whether the murders were related to some kind of violent disagreement about a drug sale. They also wondered what part, if any, the young caretaker, William Garretson, had played in the crime.

William Garretson was frightened and worried. He was confused, and his incomplete answers to their barrage of questions puzzled police. After his first interview by police, Garretson obtained Barry Tarlow as his attorney. Garretson told the police that he had had very little contact with the people who rented the main house. He worked for Rudi Altobelli. On the night of the crime, he had seen no one except a new acquaintance named Steve Parent, who had dropped by for a short visit.

Unbelievable as it seems, the LAPD did not at first connect Parent with the John Doe in the Rambler. The body was finally identified after a fingerprint of the victim was traced and the license plate number of his vehicle was checked. The Rambler belonged to Wilfred and Juanita Parent of El Monte, California. Steve Parent was their oldest son.

About the same time, following the advice of his lawyer, Barry Tarlow, William Garretson, the LAPD's prime suspect in the murders, agreed to take a polygraph (lie detector) test.

Before Garretson took the polygraph test, Sergeant Jess Buckles of the LAPD was approached by sergeants Paul Whiteley and Charles Guenther of the Los Angeles Sheriff's Office. Whiteley and Guenther were working on the Gary Hinman murder case. They thought similarities between the Hinman and Tate cases suggested a connection between the two crimes. They told Buckles about Bobby Beausoleil and his connection to a strange group of hippies living in the desert. Whiteley and Guenther felt other members of that hippie band might be involved in the Hinman crime. At that time, the police were not aware of Charles Manson's role as a cult leader.

Detective Buckles did not think the Sharon Tate murders were in any way related to the Hinman case despite the bloody words left behind at both scenes. LAPD officials still believed the Tate murders were drug related. They also thought that William Garretson's polygraph test would shed more light on the crime. At the time, they had few clues to follow. They had the knife found at the murder scene by Officer Granado. They had the unusual nylon rope that two of the victims were bound with. And they had the broken pistol grips. Blood on the grips matched Jay Sebring's blood type. They also knew that the gun used at the house was a .22 caliber revolver.

William Garretson's lie detector test was administered by Lieutenant A. H. Burdick, a polygraph expert. Burdick questioned Garretson carefully and studied the polygraph results. Lieutenant Burdick concluded without any doubt that William Garretson was in no way involved in the murders. It was his expert opinion based on facts and scientific tests.

The evening after Garretson's lie detector test, Roman Polanski arrived back in the United States. He, too, was questioned thoroughly by police. Polanski, who was very upset over the loss of his wife and unborn child, agreed to take a lie detector test at a later date.

Another Murder Scene

Fifteen-year-old Frank Struthers arrived at the home of his mother and stepfather, Rosemary and Leno LaBianca, at 8:30 A.M. on August 10, 1969. Frank had been away on a short trip. When he could not get in the house and no one answered the door, he called his twenty-one-year-old sister, Susan, from a pay phone. Susan Struthers, her brother, Frank, and her boyfriend, Joe Dorgan, went back to the LaBianca home. Using a spare pair of house keys the LaBiancas had hidden, Joe Dorgan and Frank Struthers went into the house through the back door, while Susan stayed behind. Dorgan and Struthers stumbled onto the scene of two brutal murders. They instantly called the police. Two LAPD officers arrived. The brutality of the murder scene repulsed the two policemen. It was like something from a horror movie.

Another murder investigation began. Sergeant Danny Galindo of the Robbery-Homicide Department was assigned to the case, along with Inspector K. J. McCauley. They made a detailed search of the scene and found that Rosemary LaBianca's wallet and watch were missing. However, they soon eliminated robbery as a possible motive for the crime. Too many items of value had been left behind by the intruders.

Officer Joe Granado of the SID was called to the scene and examined the murder site for blood samples. Officers Harold Dolan and J. Claborn of the SID collected fingerprints. Reports of another so-called ritual murder quickly appeared on television, on radio, and in newspapers. Wealthy people who lived in the Hollywood Hills began to fear for their lives. Everyone except the LAPD seemed to think that the Tate and LaBianca killings were linked. Celebrities in Beverly Hills believed they might be future targets of the killers.

Professional rivalry between the Los Angeles Police Department and the Los Angeles Sheriff's Office hindered the investigations in the early stages. Each department wanted to be the one to crack the high-profile cases. Instead of cooperating with each other, the departments were competitive. That competition continued to impede the investigations.

Roman Polanski became a prime focus of police questions concerning his possible involvement with the murders. Polanski suggested that he rather than his wife may have been the target of the attack. "It could be some kind of jealousy or plot or something. It couldn't be Sharon directly," he said.[2] Polanski also disputed the role drugs may have played in the crime. He swore that Sharon Tate abstained from drugs during her pregnancy. "I can tell you without question she took no drugs at all," he said.[3]

Polanski was given a polygraph test by police lieutenant Earl Deemer, which indicated that Polanski had played no part in the killings. The detectives in the Tate crime were stalled in their investigation. All they knew—based on the number of weapons used—was that the murders were not the work of a single individual. There were at least two killers involved.

One of the weapons used to commit those murders turned up on September 1, 1969. A ten-year-old boy named

Sharon Tate and her husband, director Roman Polanski, toast the opening of Polanski's film Rosemary's Baby. *At the time of Tate's death, they were eagerly awaiting the birth of her first child.*

Steven Weiss found a gun on a lawn in Sherman Oaks, California. It was a Buntline Special. The gun was rusty and had broken handle grips. The boy's father, Bernard Weiss, took great care not to pick up the gun with his bare hands. He wanted to preserve any fingerprints on it. He then called the LAPD. An officer went to Weiss's home to claim the weapon. He did not take the same care in handling the weapon used by Bernard Weiss, but held the gun with his bare hands. The gun was transported to police headquarters and filed away. No one connected it to the Tate murders. It remained out of sight and out of mind even when, days later, police officials issued a flyer describing the same make of gun as being used in the Tate crime. The Los Angeles police began a long hunt for a weapon that was already lying in the property division of a Van Nuys police station.

The Reward

Roman Polanski and a number of his celebrity friends started their own hunt for clues in the case. They posted an ad in Los Angeles newspapers:

> Reward: Roman Polanski and friends of the Polanski family offer to pay a $25,000 reward to the person or persons who furnish information leading to the arrest and conviction of the murderer or murderers of Sharon Tate, her unborn child, and the other four victims.[4]

Information on the murders would be forthcoming from an unlikely source. It would not come from someone looking to claim the reward. It would come from members of the Manson Family.

chapter four

BREAKS
IN THE CASE

INVESTIGATION—Three months had passed since the murders were committed, and the police still had no solid leads. It was luck and coincidence that provided police officers with their big break in the Tate-LaBianca cases.

In early October, police investigating an auto-theft ring raided the Barker Ranch, which was used as a headquarters by some members of the Manson Family. Manson's followers used the ranch as a site to convert stolen Volkswagens into dune buggies—off-road vehicles with large tires for use on sand. Charles Manson planned to use a fleet of dune buggies as an armada when his Helter Skelter plan began to unfold.

The police raid took place over a three-day period. Twenty-four members of the Manson Family were arrested, including Susan Atkins and Manson himself.

While the raid was going on, two young women jumped out of some bushes where they were hiding and asked police officers for protection. They told police they wanted to leave the Family and feared for their lives. One of the women was named Stephanie Schram. The other was Kitty Lutesinger. Seventeen-year-old Kitty Lutesinger was the girlfriend of Bobby Beausoleil. Beausoleil was under arrest as the prime suspect in the Gary Hinman murder case. Police sergeants Paul Whiteley and Charles Guenther of the LASO had been looking for Kitty Lutesinger. She was wanted for questioning in the Hinman case.

Whiteley and Guenther questioned Kitty Lutesinger, who was eager to tell all she knew. She claimed that while living at the ranch, she had heard that Charles Manson sent Bobby Beausoleil and a woman named Susan Atkins to the home of Gary Hinman to collect some money. When Hinman refused to turn over the money, there was a fight, and Hinman was killed. Lutesinger did not recall who had told her about the incident, but she did provide some additional information. Lutesinger had heard from Susan Atkins herself that she had been in a fight with a man who pulled her hair. In retaliation, Atkins had stabbed the man in the legs a number of times with a Buck knife.

Officers Whiteley and Guenther knew that Gary Hinman had not been stabbed in the legs. They were not sure what to do with that bit of information, so they filed it away for future reference. Perhaps it related to the victim of another crime Atkins was involved in. At that point, the investigators were not sure.

However, more information was coming into the Los Angeles Sheriff's Office. In mid-October of that year, the

LAPD and LASO finally agreed to pool their clues and resources in the multiple murder investigations. Detectives of the LAPD were finally considering the possibility that all of the murders could have been related. Kitty Lutesinger's information suggested to the police that the band of hippies running a stolen car ring from the Barker and Spahn ranches may be involved in more serious crimes. After all, the police knew that Voytek Frykowski, one of the people killed at the Polanski home in Beverly Hills, had been stabbed in the legs numerous times. Was Frykowski the man Susan Atkins had told Kitty Lutesinger about? Detectives Whiteley and Guenther decided to question Susan Atkins.

Susan Atkins was being held under the name Sadie Mae Glutz during the raid of the Barker Ranch. The officers of the sheriff's department tracked her down and questioned her in jail.

Susan Atkins proved to be a very talkative person. She admitted going with Bobby Beausoleil to the home of Gary Hinman. Atkins claimed she had helped Beausoleil hold Hinman hostage when he refused to give them money. She also admitted that she had been there when Bobby Beausoleil killed Gary Hinman. Susan Atkins did not implicate Charles Manson in the crime, nor did she admit to helping Beausoleil perform the actual murder. When the officers asked Atkins to repeat her tale on tape, she refused. They booked her on suspicion of murder.

At that point, there still was no real connection between the Hinman murder and the Tate and LaBianca murders. All that the police had was a hunch that the man Susan Atkins

Charles Manson persuaded Arlene Barker to let the Family live on her ranch in the remote California desert. Shown here is the breezeway of the ranch house, littered with trash.

said she had stabbed in the legs could be Voytek Frykowski. Officers Whiteley and Guenther continued to follow up on the hunch.

Once again, they interviewed Kitty Lutesinger, who had been released into the custody of her parents. They also began to accumulate a list of people associated with Susan Atkins and the Manson Family. Kitty Lutesinger helped in that chore. She told the investigators that Charles Manson had dealings with a motorcycle gang known as the Straight Satans. One of those gang members, a biker named Danny, had become quite friendly with Charles and other Family members.

The detectives interviewed members of the Straight

Satans motorcycle gang. A gang member named Al Springer told the investigators that when he visited the Spahn Ranch in August, Manson had bragged to him about killing five people. Springer added that Manson also said that the group had written something in blood on the refrigerator at the scene of one crime. The words written at the scene had something to do with pigs. The biker's story aroused the interest of the detectives. A reference to pigs had been left at all three murder scenes, and at the LaBianca house, words had been written on the refrigerator.

The investigators then discovered that the Danny mentioned by Kitty Lutesinger was Straight Satans gang member Danny DeCarlo. Whiteley and Guenther went to interview DeCarlo who told them that a Manson Family member named Clem (Steve Grogan) had also bragged about killing five people. Clem had used the word "piggies" to describe the victims, he said.

DeCarlo also said that the day after the Tate murders, he had heard that the Family was involved in the murder of Gary Hinman and in the disappearance of a man named Donald Shea. Shea, who was known by the nickname "Shorty," worked as a hand on the Spahn Ranch. When Shorty threatened to tell ranch owner George Spahn about the illegal activities of the Family, Charles Manson had him killed. According to DeCarlo, Family member Bruce Davis had told him about the murder and joked about cutting Shorty's body into pieces so he could not be identified.

DeCarlo provided another important link between the Manson Family and the murders. He said Charles Manson had a .22 caliber Buntline Special that he sometimes carried around in a holster. Members of the Family used the handgun for target practice at the ranch.

Officers Whiteley and Guenther shared their new information with officers of the Los Angeles Police Department. LAPD detectives listened to the report, but they were not totally convinced that a connection between the Manson Family and all of the murders existed.

Detectives from the LASO were not as dubious. They were now sure that Charles Manson and his followers had something to do with not only the Hinman killing, but also the Tate and LaBianca murders.

Atkins Talks Too Much

Susan Atkins was being held at the Sybil Brand Women's House of Detention in Los Angeles. In jail, Atkins did not seem to be alarmed by the serious charges against her. She treated her imprisonment like a joke and spent much of her time dancing around her cell and singing. Atkins became friendly with two of her cell mates. One was Ronnie Howard, a former prostitute who was jailed for forging a prescription. The other was Virginia Graham, also a prostitute, who was in jail for parole violations.

Atkins loved to talk. She talked about everything from psychic phenomena to a man named Charles Manson who Atkins believed was Jesus Christ. Howard and Graham listened to the endless chatter of their young cell mate. One day, Susan Atkins's talk turned to a more serious topic—murder.

Susan Atkins matter-of-factly told Virginia Graham that she was accused of killing Gary Hinman.

"Did you do it?" Graham asked her.

"Sure," Susan Atkins replied without hesitation.[1] Atkins went on to explain more about her part in the crime. She said the cops had it backward. They thought her friend Bobby Beausoleil stabbed Hinman while Atkins held down the victim. It was really the other way around. Beausoleil held down Hinman and Atkins herself stabbed him.

At first, Ronnie Howard and Virginia Graham thought Susan Atkins—or "Sadie," as she liked to be called—was just nutty. They did not know if she was telling the truth or making up wild stories.

Meanwhile, some Manson Family members taken in the raid on the Barker Ranch had been released for lack of evidence. Others were still jailed. Among those remaining in jail were Charles Manson and a woman who told police her name was Leslie Sankston. Leslie Sankston was really Leslie Van Houten. Detectives investigating the LaBianca murders questioned Sankston and Manson about the murders. One of the detectives asked Manson if he knew anything about the Tate or LaBianca murders. Charles Manson calmly denied knowing anything about either crime.

Another detective questioned Leslie Sankston about the Tate-LaBianca murders. Sankston claimed to know little about the crimes. However, she did admit that she knew Susan Atkins. She also said someone connected with the Manson Family might be involved in the Tate crime, but she could not be certain. The interviews shed no light on the investigation.

More Jailhouse Talk

Inmate Virginia Graham listened in astonishment one day as her cell mate, Susan Atkins, began to talk in detail about the Sharon Tate murder. The conversation began on November 6, 1969.

"You know who did it, don't you?" Atkins asked her. Virginia Graham said that she did not know. "Well, you're looking at her," Susan Atkins answered.[2]

Atkins went on to explain just how the murders had been committed. She explained the gruesome details coolly and calmly as if devoid of any feelings of guilt or remorse. One by one, she told how each victim perished. Atkins talked the most about Sharon Tate and how she begged for her life. She repeated Tate's pleas to Graham.

"Please don't kill me. Please don't kill me. I don't want to die. I want to live. I want to have my baby. I want to have my baby." Atkins was unmoved by Tate's words. She said she had told her, "You're going to die, and I don't feel anything about it."[3]

Virginia Graham was horrified by Atkins's cold-blooded account of the crime. She asked Susan Atkins if killing a pregnant woman bothered her.

Susan Atkins admitted that it did not affect her in the least. She told Graham it was just part of Helter Skelter. Virginia Graham did not know what Susan Atkins meant. Atkins went on to add that after the killings were done, she had left her bloody handprint behind and had also lost her knife. She had wanted to go back to look for the knife, but did not. Susan Atkins then told Graham how the group committed more murders the next day and got rid of their bloody clothes by throwing them down a ravine.

While in jail, Susan Atkins rambled on and on about the Family's crime spree. In addition to the Hinman, Tate, and LaBianca murders, she said three other bodies were buried out in the desert. She also revealed that the Family had a list of celebrities marked for death in the near future. The intended victims included Academy Award-winning actors Elizabeth Taylor and Richard Burton, actor Steve McQueen, superstar Frank Sinatra, and singer Tom Jones. Atkins repeated her tale of murder to Ronnie Howard a bit later. Graham and Howard discussed their cell mate's story. They decided Susan Atkins was either a nutty liar or a dia-

bolical killer. When Virginia Graham was transferred to another prison, she was relieved to part company with Susan Atkins. Once Virginia Graham and Ronnie Howard were separated, they gave deep thought to the

The famous singer Frank Sinatra, along with several other celebrities, was targeted by the Manson Family.

confessions of their young cell mate. Both women decided to share the story with police officials. At first, prison officials would not permit the two women to talk with representatives of the LAPD. Several days passed.

On November 17, 1969, Ronnie Howard was granted permission to speak with two LAPD detectives. She repeated to them Susan Atkins's chilling tale of multiple murder. In talking to Ronnie Howard, Susan Atkins had implicated herself and Charles Manson in the Tate-LaBianca murders. Atkins was already involved in the Hinman murder case, which was ready to go to trial. Kitty Lutesinger, Al Springer, and Danny DeCarlo had also made connections between the Manson Family and the crimes (although the two men had not agreed to testify in court). Other evidence was also accumulating. It was time for the wheels of justice to be put into motion. Helping to keep those wheels in motion would be some surprise witnesses who would agree to testify against Charles Manson and members of his cult Family.

chapter five

THE PROSECUTION PREPARES

CALIFORNIA, 1969—At the time of the murders, Vincent Bugliosi was a thirty-five-year-old deputy district attorney for Los Angeles. District attorneys are government lawyers who present the state's case for conviction of a crime against the defendant before a jury. They use the evidence gathered by police. On November 18, 1969, Bugliosi was given the difficult job of preparing a case against Charles Manson and his Family. It was Bugliosi's task to prove that Manson and some of his followers were responsible for the deaths of Sharon Tate, Jay Sebring, Abigail Folger, Voytek Frykowski, Steve Parent, Leno LaBianca, and Rosemary LaBianca.

Since Charles Manson was not present at the time of the murders, Bugliosi had to prove that Manson ordered his followers to commit the crimes. In addition, he had to show that while the members were directed by Manson to act, they were not mindless zombies acting without reason or forethought. Vincent Bugliosi had to establish that Susan Atkins, Charles "Tex" Watson, Patricia Krenwinkel, Linda Kasabian, and Leslie Van Houten were willing participants in a conspiracy to commit murder and in the actual act of murder itself.

Vincent Bugliosi was confident that he could prosecute the case successfully. In 104 previous felony jury trials, he had lost only one case. He was also well supported on the case by deputy district attorneys Steven Kay and Donald Musich. Together the three prosecutors took on a case that would last almost two years. It would result in a marathon nine-month trial that at the time was the most expensive trial in U.S. legal history.

Sorting Out Evidence

One of the first things that Vincent Bugliosi did was to participate in searches of the Spahn and Barker ranches. The searches turned up a pair of heavy-duty wire cutters that were found in a dune buggy belonging to Charles Manson. Police officials thought the wire cutters may have been used to cut the phone lines at the Polanski home. At the Spahn Ranch, police researchers carefully gathered up .22 caliber bullets and empty .22 caliber shell casings left in a canyon where Manson and his followers frequently held target practice.

The police were informed of the target range by motorcycle gang member Danny DeCarlo. He also provided links between the Manson Family and several weapons used in the murders. He told police about a Buntline Special used by the Family; that type of gun was one of the weapons

Deputy District Attorney Vincent Bugliosi answers questions for the media. Bugliosi had the challenging task of prosecuting the murder case against Manson and several members of his cult Family.

used in the Tate murders. DeCarlo described a sword owned by Manson. It had been used to slice off part of Gary Hinman's ear. In addition, DeCarlo mentioned a type of knife normally carried by Family member Susan Atkins. Atkins carried a small Buck knife like the one found at the Tate murder scene.

Danny DeCarlo also told police officials that Charles Manson had bought long lengths of an unusual type of three-strand rope for use at the ranch. It was the same type of rope used to tie up Sharon Tate and Jay Sebring.

The motorcycle gang member provided an even more startling final bit of information to police: He told officers that Bobby Beausoleil had personally confessed to him that he had stabbed Gary Hinman. Danny DeCarlo agreed to testify in the Hinman murder trial, which was already going on, in exchange for having some old charges of theft dropped.

Danny DeCarlo was not the only source of information. Leslie Van Houten revealed in a police interview that three women had gone to the Tate house on the night of the murder. Van Houten provided that information after she learned Susan Atkins was already talking about the crime. Van Houten also said one of the women—Linda—did not kill anyone.

One by one, other Manson Family members came forward with bits and pieces of information. A woman named Barbara Hoyt who had left the Family told the police about a night of murder in the desert. Hoyt said she had heard Shorty Shea screaming one night. The next day he was gone, and she never saw him again.

One of the Family's first members, a woman named Mary Brunner, added more information about Shorty Shea. Brunner was involved in the Hinman case—she had gone to Hinman's house with Susan Atkins and Bobby Beausoleil on the day of the stabbing. Mary Brunner cooperated with police in exchange for immunity in the Hinman murder. (Having immunity means that a person will not be prosecuted for involvement in a case if he or she agrees to testify for the prosecution.) Brunner said that Charles "Tex" Watson had bragged to her about Shorty's murder. Watson described how it was done and where the body was buried. Shea's car was also stolen. Brunner told police where Family members had dumped the stolen vehicle.

The district attorney's office had Ronnie Howard's account of the murders based on what Susan Atkins had told her. Law enforcement officers had now identified the five people involved in committing the Tate-LaBianca murders: Susan Atkins, Tex Watson, Patricia Krenwinkel, Linda Kasabian, and Leslie Van Houten.

Fingerprint evidence was also starting to turn up. One of Charles "Tex" Watson's fingerprints had been found on the front door of the Polanski-Tate home. Another print belonging to Patricia Krenwinkel was found on a door leading to Sharon Tate's bedroom. The prints matched with ones taken from Manson Family members during prior run-ins with the law for minor crimes.

Warrants were issued for the five Manson Family members involved in the Tate-LaBianca murders. Susan Atkins and Leslie Van Houten were already in custody in

California. Patricia Krenwinkel was apprehended in Mobile, Alabama. Linda Kasabian, who was in Concord, New Hampshire, voluntarily surrendered to police. She admitted she was at the scenes of the crimes, but she said she did not participate in the murders. Charles "Tex" Watson had fled to his hometown of McKinney, Texas, where he had grown up as a local sports star. In fact, Watson's second cousin, Tom Montgomery, was the local sheriff. Tex Watson was taken into custody in Texas. However, there was some question about the willingness of officials in Texas to return Watson to California in order to stand trial.

In December 1969, attorney Richard Caballero, who was representing Susan Atkins, met with the prosecuting attorneys to work out a deal. He brought with him a taped confession made by Atkins. On the tape, Susan Atkins repeated the tale she has told to Virginia Graham and Ronnie Howard. It was agreed that if Atkins testified truthfully in the Hinman, Tate, and LaBianca cases, the prosecution would not ask for the death penalty for her. It was also agreed that if Atkins for any reason refused to testify later at her trial, the testimony she gave to the grand jury would not be used against her.

The Long Road to Court

On December 5, 1969, Susan Atkins testified before the grand jury, which would decide if there was enough evidence to bring her to trial. The grand jury hears only the state's evidence, in order to decide whether someone should be indicted; the defense does not present a case. Atkins told

Linda Kasabian and Leslie Van Houten leave the courtroom after hearings on December 22, 1969. Kasabian told investigators she was at the scene of the crimes but did not participate in the murders.

the twisted tale of two nights of brutal, senseless murder. She explained the parts she played in the crimes. She also described the roles of Charles Manson and fellow Manson followers Tex Watson, Patricia Krenwinkel, Linda Kasabian, and Leslie Van Houten. It was bloodcurdling testimony delivered in a matter-of-fact monotone. Atkins showed no remorse or sorrow.

After Atkins's testimony, Gary Fleischman, who was Linda Kasabian's attorney, went to Deputy District Attorney Vincent Bugliosi seeking to make a deal for his client. Bugliosi said a deal might be worked out at a later date.

Fingerprint experts then testified before the grand jury. A police sergeant testified about the .22 caliber Buntline Special gun grips found at the Tate crime scene. A Hollywood agent told the grand jury about Charles Manson's connection to the house once owned by Terry Melcher. A police officer testified regarding the nylon rope, the blood on the broken gun grips, and the finding of the Buck knife.

Next, biker Danny DeCarlo took the stand. He talked about seeing the .22 caliber Buntline Special at the Spahn Ranch along with the three-strand nylon rope like that used in the Tate murders.

It took only twenty minutes of deliberation for the grand jury to reach a decision. They returned indictments of murder. Leslie Van Houten was charged with two counts of murder and one count of conspiracy to commit murder. Charles Manson, Susan Atkins, Charles "Tex" Watson, and Linda Kasabian were each charged with seven counts of murder and one count of conspiracy to commit murder. The grand jury had decided that there was sufficient evidence for all of the accused to stand trial.

Arraignment

In December 1969, the defendants were brought into court to answer the indictments handed down by the grand jury. It was their chance to plead guilty or not guilty to the charges. Presiding over the arraignment was Judge William Keene. Susan Atkins, Leslie Van Houten, and Linda Kasabian appeared in court on December 10. All three requested and were granted continuances (adjournments) before entering their pleas. They needed more time to make up their minds about the form their defenses would take. On December 11, 1969, Charles Manson was brought before Judge Keene. At the time, Manson did not have the money to hire an attorney. He was represented by Paul Fitzgerald of the public defender's office. He, too, was allowed to postpone entering his plea.

Press and television coverage of the case was now worldwide. Even high political officials in Washington, D.C., were talking about the Charles Manson Family and the Tate-LaBianca murders.

On December 16, 1969, Susan Atkins returned to court and pleaded not guilty to all counts against her. On December 17, 1969, Charles Manson was back in court to plead not guilty. He also asked Judge Keene to dismiss his public defender. Charles Manson wanted to defend himself. Judge Keene was not sure Manson could do an adequate job.

Manson replied:

> Your Honor, there is no way I can give up my voice in this matter. If I can't speak, then our whole thing is done. If I can't speak in my own defense and converse freely in this courtroom, then it ties my hands behind my back, and if I have no voice, then there is no sense in having a defense.[1]

Charles Manson seemed to be bright, rational, and well-spoken at that time. Judge Keene agreed to consider Manson's request.

On December 19, 1969, Leslie Van Houten stood in court and asked Judge Keene to replace her attorney, Donald Barnett. Keene dismissed Barnett and appointed Marvin Part as Van Houten's lawyer. She, too, pleaded not guilty.

Patricia Krenwinkel, Tex Watson, and Linda Kasabian had not yet entered their pleas. Krenwinkel was still in Alabama awaiting extradition to California. (Extradition is the turning over of an accused person or fugitive from one state, country, or jurisdiction to another to stand trial.) Tex Watson remained in custody in Texas, and with the help of his attorney, Bill Boyd, he planned to fight extradition.

Linda Kasabian was already trying to make a deal with the prosecution. Since she had played no active part in the actual murders, she was willing to testify against her former Family members in exchange for immunity. On January 6, 1970, Linda Kasabian pleaded not guilty to the charges against her.

More Evidence

Police were unable to locate the bloody clothing thrown away by the murderers and the gun used by Tex Watson at the Tate house. After Susan Atkins's confession appeared in the newspapers, a television crew from KABC–TV Channel 7 set out to find the clothing. Using clues and descriptions given by Atkins, the TV crew managed to find the location that Atkins said had "a mountain on one side and a ravine on the other."[2] The crew led the real detectives to the spot, and the bloody clothing was recovered.

An additional piece of evidence also turned up after the indictments were handed down. Rosemary LaBianca's wallet was found in a restroom at a gas station where the killers had left it.

Another crucial piece of evidence was discovered after the grand jury decision. Bernard Weiss, the father of the boy who had found the broken .22 Buntline Special and turned it in to the police, read about the indictments in the newspaper. He called the LAPD homicide division to inquire if the gun his son had found was the murder weapon. He was told that old guns turned into the police were not kept long and usually ended up being destroyed.

"I can't believe that you'd throw away what could be the single most important piece of evidence in the Tate case!" Weiss exclaimed.[3]

Bernard Weiss called a television newscaster. The newscaster phoned the LAPD. The police looked for the gun Weiss had turned in and located it in a police property room. A man named Randy Starr then came forward. Starr told police he was the man who had originally owned the .22 caliber Buntline Special. Randy Starr had given the gun to Charles Manson. Evidence was piling up connecting Charles Manson to the crimes.

A sixteen-year-old Family member named Dianne Lake gave police more evidence of Leslie Van Houten's involvement in the LaBianca murders. In August 1969, Van Houten had told Lake that she had stabbed someone who was already dead. Van Houten had told Lake that the murder was committed near Griffith Park (in the area where the actual crime occurred).

Lake told police that according to Leslie Van Houten, when the crime was over, the killers had written words in blood on a refrigerator door in the victim's kitchen. Dianne Lake added one final comment. Leslie Van Houten told her a big boat was parked outside of the house where the murder was committed. Police knew that Leno LaBianca's boat had been parked in the driveway after the LaBiancas returned from their short vacation trip. Pieces of the crime puzzle were starting to fit together. However, the entire picture was not yet complete.

The First Hinman Murder Trial

The first trial of Bobby Beausoleil for the murder of Gary Hinman began in November 1969. Beausoleil was represented by attorney Leon Salter. The case for the prosecution was weak. At the time, investigators were still collecting clues in the Tate-LaBianca murders. Much of what they learned shed light on the Hinman murder.

The original case against Beausoleil was based on the fact that Beausoleil was caught driving one of Hinman's cars. A knife believed to be the murder weapon was in the car. Beausoleil's clothing had dried bloodstains on them—the same type as Hinman's blood.

The police interview of gang member Danny DeCarlo took place while the Hinman case was being tried. When the police found out that Beausoleil had confessed to DeCarlo that he had committed the murder, DeCarlo was rushed into court to testify. On the witness stand, DeCarlo was unprepared and seemed unreliable. The jury could not reach a unanimous decision to convict or acquit Bobby Beausoleil. On November 28, 1969, they were declared to be a hung jury (one that cannot reach a decision). A new trial was set. Beausoleil was confident he would later be acquitted and freed. He told friends he planned to start his own Manson-like Family after his eventual release.

At the time of the Beausoleil trial, Deputy District Attorney Vincent Bugliosi was deeply involved in the Tate-LaBianca trial. Nevertheless, he agreed to take over the prosecution of Bobby Beausoleil. The retrial was set for February 9, 1970. However, Judge Keene later set the trial date for Susan Atkins in the Tate-LaBianca case for the same day. Bugliosi was taken off the Beausoleil case and it was assigned to Deputy District Attorney Burton Katz.

The Path to Trial

In January 1970, attorney Marvin Part requested that a court-appointed psychiatrist examine his client, Leslie Van

Houten. However, Van Houten did not want to be examined or evaluated, because she did not want to consider an insanity plea as a defense tactic. (An insanity plea is based on the claim that the accused did not have the mental capability to know the difference between right and wrong or to understand the crime. Defendants who are deemed insane at the time of a crime cannot be executed, and they serve time in an institution for the criminally insane rather than a regular prison.) Charles Manson heard about the request for a psychiatric evaluation through prison gossip. Through Lynette "Squeaky" Fromme, a frequent visitor to other Family members, Manson sent a message to Leslie Van Houten urging her to fire her current attorney and use attorney Ira Reiner instead. (Manson had talked to Reiner a number of times but had never been represented by him.) Van Houten obeyed Manson's order. She requested that Marvin Part be removed as her counsel and that attorney Ira Reiner take his place. Marvin Part in turn argued that Manson was controlling his client's will and asked not to be removed.

Judge George Dell received Van Houten's request and considered the arguments. After questioning Ira Reiner, Judge Dell allowed Leslie Van Houten to replace Part with Reiner.

Charles Manson's plan was becoming apparent. He wanted a joint trial of all the defendants. If they were tried jointly, the prosecution would have to prove that all the defendants were guilty. If one was acquitted, they would all go free. Manson did not want separate trials. His idea would work only if all of the Family members, including Bobby Beausoleil, stuck together. Beausoleil understood Manson's logic, but he decided to keep his lawyer, Léon Salter.

Patricia Krenwinkel was a willing partner to Manson's scheme. She returned to California and pleaded not guilty. She was later defended by attorney Paul Fitzgerald (Charles Manson's first lawyer), who quit the public defender's office to represent her.

Charles "Tex" Watson, with the help of his attorney, decided to fight extradition. It appeared that most of the female defendants were still willing to follow their leader, but male Family members were beginning to question the decisions of Charles Manson. One of the women who was not willing to go along with Charles Manson was Linda Kasabian.

A New Star Witness

Linda Kasabian and her attorney, Gary Fleischman, were anxious to make a deal with the prosecutors. Vincent Bugliosi wanted to make a deal with Linda Kasabian. After all, Kasabian might be the least guilty of the Manson Family members involved in the crimes. She had done nothing to prevent the murders, but she had not personally killed anyone either. The problem was, a deal was already in the works with Susan Atkins, who was a confessed murderer. Atkins had agreed to talk to save herself from the death penalty. The prosecution could not make two deals at the same time.

There was another problem with the Susan Atkins deal.

Patricia Krenwinkel, who had left a fingerprint at the Tate murder scene, fled to Alabama. She was captured in Mobile and taken back to California to stand trial.

If Atkins changed her mind and refused to testify at the trial, the actual case against Linda Kasabian would be very weak. It was likely that Kasabian would be acquitted. Without Atkins's testimony to implicate her, Linda Kasabian would not need a deal to help her avoid prosecution.

Another problem with the deal was that the prosecution really needed the testimony of Linda Kasabian to strengthen their case if indeed Susan Atkins did change her mind at the last minute. However, then it would be too late to make a deal with Kasabian. What could the prosecution offer Kasabian to testify? The situation was as serious as it was confusing.

Kasabian was an accessory to murder. (An accessory is someone who is not present when a crime is committed but is guilty of the crime by instigating, concealing, or giving advice about it.) She wanted immunity in exchange for her testimony against the other Family members. Of course, if Susan Atkins went back on her deal, Linda Kasabian might be acquitted, which would be better from her point of view. The hands of the prosecution were tied. It was Susan Atkins who untied the hands of Vincent Bugliosi and solved the problem.

After numerous visits from other Manson Family members, Atkins called in her attorney, Richard Caballero. She told him that under no circumstances would she testify at the trial. Caballero contacted Bugliosi's office and told him the news. The deal was off. The prosecutors then called Gary Fleischman, Linda Kasabian's lawyer, to make a deal. Kasabian was offered immunity from prosecution in exchange for her testimony. An additional item was added to the agreement: If she did not testify truthfully or changed her mind about testifying, she would be fully prosecuted and any information she had previously given to the prosecution would be used against her.

Now the prosecution was ready to go to court.

chapter six

THE TRIAL

COURTROOM—The lengthy merry-go-round of switching defense attorneys continued as the official date for the murder trial to begin neared. Judge William Keene had taken over the case once again, replacing Judge Dell. Keene granted Charles Manson permission to meet with Susan Atkins to prepare his defense. After Manson's visit, Susan Atkins fired her attorney, Richard Caballero. He was replaced by attorney Daye Shinn.

A short time later, Charles Manson appeared in court before Judge Keene to make some requests. Most of them were outlandish. Manson wanted to be released from custody. He felt he should be free to travel wherever he wanted in order to prepare his defense.

Judge Keene denied the request. He also told Manson it was becoming clear that he was incapable of acting as his own attorney. The remark angered Manson.

"It's not me that's on trial here as much as this court is on trial," Manson raged. He then looked at Judge Keene and said, "Go wash your hands! They're dirty."

Judge Keene had had enough of Manson's outbursts and outrageous comments. Said the judge, "Mr. Manson, your status, at this time, of acting as your own attorney is now vacated!"[1]

Judge Keene then appointed Charles Hollopeter to be Manson's defense attorney. The judge added that if Manson found another lawyer he liked better, Hollopeter would be replaced.

A Circus Atmosphere

Charles Manson became a notorious celebrity. His unruly antics were widely publicized by the press. He became something of a cult hero, even though he was suspected of masterminding mass murders and attempting to start a race war. Women wrote to Manson, begging to join his Family. His face was pictured on the front pages of newspapers and on the covers of top magazines. The Manson Family received continuous coverage from TV news shows. The Manson women were interviewed so often that they were on a first-name basis with many reporters. People everywhere were talking about Charles Manson and his followers. The case was even discussed in the White House (as will be shown later).

On March 19, 1970, Charles Hollopeter requested that his client, Charles Manson, be given a psychiatric examination. Manson refused and dismissed Hollopeter. Charles Hollopeter was replaced by Ronald Hughes, who was more to Manson's liking. Ronald Hughes was not a typical suit-and-tie lawyer. He wore hip, young clothing. His lifestyle was unconventional. He identified himself with America's new youth movement. The press referred to him as a hippie lawyer.

Charles Manson was now content with his defense team. Susan Atkins was represented by Daye Shinn. Leslie Van Houten had Ira Reiner as her attorney. Patricia Krenwinkel was defended by Paul Fitzgerald. It was a group of lawyers that Manson thought he could dominate. Charles Manson planned to call his own legal shots in court.

A New Case

The retrial of Bobby Beausoleil for the murder of Gary Hinman began in March 1970. This time the prosecution, led by Burton Katz, had a stronger case. The difference was the testimony of Mary Brunner. Brunner's and Danny DeCarlo's testimony, along with the other evidence, helped convict Beausoleil. The prosecution asked for the death penalty in the case and got it. Bobby Beausoleil was sentenced to die.

Danny DeCarlo and Mary Brunner also testified before the grand jury in the Gary Hinman murder case. The result was that additional charges were brought against Susan Atkins, Charles Manson, and Bruce Davis in the case. It was not long afterward that Bruce Davis dropped out of sight.

In April 1970, Charles Manson filed an affidavit of prejudice against Judge William Keene. A defendant may

Charles Manson sticks out his tongue at photographers as he sits in a courtroom. Manson's unusual actions and bizarre requests led to a circuslike atmosphere in court.

file such a challenge to have a judge removed without giving any reason for the challenge. Judge Keene was taken off the case, and the Manson murder trial was reassigned to Judge Charles H. Older. In May of that same year, Susan Atkins filed a legal declaration repudiating (denying) her grand jury testimony about the Tate and LaBianca murders. The filing of the declaration meant that all prior deals with the prosecution were officially off once and for all. Atkins could not change her mind again. She would face the death penalty if convicted.

Bobby Beausoleil then produced an affidavit (an oath in writing) signed by Mary Brunner. In the affidavit, Brunner claimed her testimony at Beausoleil's trial was false. Brunner said she had lied when she said Beausoleil had stabbed Hinman to death. Called back into court, Mary Brunner repudiated her repudiation—that is, now she was saying that Beausoleil *did* stab Hinman. It was very confusing, especially to the prosecuting attorney, Burton Katz. One thing was clear: Since Mary Brunner had been granted immunity from prosecution after the Beausoleil case, she was safe. Only a charge of perjury (giving false testimony under oath) could be brought against her. While legal minds tried to unravel the truth, Bobby Beausoleil remained in San Quentin Prison.

Charles Manson and Susan Atkins were then brought before Judge George Dell to answer new charges brought against them in the Hinman case. Once again, Manson asked to handle his own defense. His request was denied, and he selected Irving Kanarek to defend him. Daye Shinn

Charles Manson walks into court to enter his plea in the Gary Hinman murder trial. Also being tried is Susan Atkins (seated).

represented Susan Atkins. Irving Kanarek replaced Ronald Hughes as Manson's lawyer, but Hughes was not done with the case. Leslie Van Houten picked him to replace Ira Reiner as her attorney.

The Case Proceeds

Legal efforts to extradite Charles "Tex" Watson from Texas to California became bogged down. Rather than wait until Watson was returned to the state where he was charged with murder, the prosecution decided to proceed with the case without Watson's presence. Charles Manson, Susan Atkins, Patricia Krenwinkel, and Leslie Van Houten finally got their day in court. The Tate-LaBianca trial officially began on June 15, 1970. It quickly became a stage for bizarre performances by Charles Manson and his three female followers.

The first example of Manson's rebellious attitude in court came early in the trial. While sitting in court, Charles Manson suddenly turned his chair so his back was facing Judge Older.

"The Court has shown me no respect," Manson explained, "so I am going to show the Court the same thing."[2] Manson refused to turn and face forward. After several warnings, bailiffs removed him from the courtroom. When Susan Atkins, Patricia Krenwinkel, and Leslie Van Houten faced Judge Older in court, they followed Manson's example. They stood up and turned their backs to Judge Older in defiance of his authority. They, too, were removed from the courtroom.

The next day, all of the defendants were back in court. Judge Older warned the defendants that performing such acts in front of a jury might prejudice the jury against them.

In response, Manson stood up and went into a crucifixion pose, his arms stretched out to the side. The women quickly copied his pose. All four stood there as if they were being crucified. Again, the four defendants were removed from the courtroom by guards.

Jury selection in the Tate-LaBianca case was not an easy process. Jurors had to prove they could make a fair and impartial decision based solely on the evidence presented in court. They also had to realize that the defendants had to be proven guilty by the prosecutors. It was not the job of the defense team to prove the innocence of their clients. The burden of proof was on the prosecution.

Other factors also made jury selection most difficult. When the first twelve potential jurors were asked if sitting on the jury for six months or more would cause any of them a hardship, eight raised their hands and were excused. It was the start of a mass exodus of potential jurors. The prosecutors and each attorney for the defense had the right to challenge the ability of any potential juror to render a fair and honest verdict in the case. Some potential jurors were afraid of retaliation by the Manson Family and were excused. Other jurors revealed that they did not personally favor the death penalty and were excused at the request of the prosecutors. Anyone who had read Susan Atkins's confession, which had been printed in the newspapers, was excused. Lawyers for the defense felt they were already prejudiced in the case. On July 14, 1970, a jury of twelve was accepted by both the prosecution and the defense. The jury consisted of seven men and five women ranging in age from twenty-five to seventy-five.

The jury consisted of John Baer, an electrical tester; Alva Dawson, a retired deputy sheriff; Shirley Evans, a school secretary; Evelyn Hines, a dictaphone operator; William McBride II, a chemical company employee; Thelma McKenzie, a clerical supervisor; Marie Mesmer, a drama critic; Jean Roseland, an executive secretary; Anlee Sisto, an electronics technician; Herman Tubick, a mortician; Walter Vitzelio, a retired plant guard; and William Zamora, a highway engineer.

In addition to the twelve jurors, six alternate jurors were selected. Alternate jurors sit through the entire trial, but do not take part in the deliberation or vote on the verdict. They are present to fill a spot if a regular juror is unable to serve the conclusion of the trial. The six alternate jurors for the trial were Frances Chasen, a retired civil servant; Kenneth Daut, Jr., a state highway employee; Robert Douglass, an employee of the Army Corps of Engineers; John Ellis, a telephone installer; Victoria Kampman, a housewife; and Larry Sheely, a telephone maintenance man. Opening statements in the Tate-LaBianca trial were begun on July 24, 1970. In his opening statement, Prosecutor Vincent Bugliosi described Charles Manson as a

> vagrant wanderer, a frustrated singer-guitarist . . . who would refer to himself as Jesus Christ . . . and was a killer

who cleverly masqueraded behind the common image of a hippie, that of being peace loving . . . but was a megalomaniac who coupled his insatiable thirst for power with an intense obsession for violent death.[3]

(A megalomaniac is one who attributes great importance to himself.)

Bugliosi went on to announce that his principal witness would be Linda Kasabian, a Family member who accompanied the killers to both the Tate and LaBianca murders. Bugliosi told the jury Manson had a motive for the seemingly senseless crimes. He claimed it was a motive even stranger than the murders themselves.

Charles Manson had his own way of greeting the jury and the press on that day. Manson appeared in court with a large, bloody X carved into his forehead. The cult leader explained what the mark on his forehead meant.

"I have X'ed myself from your world," Manson said.[4] The next day, Susan Atkins, Patricia Krenwinkel, and Leslie Van Houten appeared in court with X's carved on their foreheads.

The free members of the Manson Family also followed Charles Manson's example. They, too, carved X's into their foreheads. It was Lynette "Squeaky" Fromme who helped hold the Family together by acting as the leader in Manson's absence.

"I'll die for Charlie," Fromme admitted to reporters who asked about the X on her forehead. "I'll kill for him. I'll do whatever is necessary."[5]

Manson's next act of defiance was to alter the X on his

At the beginning of his trial for the Tate-LaBianca murders, Manson appeared in court with a bloody X carved into his forehead. He announced that he had done it himself.

forehead. He cut it into a Nazi swastika. Susan Atkins, Patricia Krenwinkel, and Leslie Van Houten followed suit. Free members of the Manson Family also cut swastikas on their foreheads.

Strange goings-on continued both inside and outside the courtroom. Outside, Manson Family members staged demonstrations to support Manson. Some of his women crawled on their hands and knees for miles along a paved main road to make the public aware of Manson's plight. However, not all of the demonstrations and acts were nonviolent.

Barbara Hoyt, a former Family member who was a witness for the prosecution, was lured to Hawaii by Manson followers. They then fed Hoyt a hamburger laced with a large dose of LSD, hoping to kill her. It did not. Barbara Hoyt had to be hospitalized, but she survived.

Linda Kasabian Testifies

Prosecutor Vincent Bugliosi called his star witness, Linda Kasabian, to the stand on July 27, 1970. She would eventually remain on the stand for eighteen days, including seven days of cross-examination. (Cross-examination is questioning by lawyers for the other side.) Kasabian was asked by Bugliosi why she chose to testify in addition to the fact that she would receive immunity from prosecution for doing so.

"I strongly believe in the truth," said Kasabian, "and I feel the truth should be spoken."[6]

Linda Kasabian went on to tell the stories of the

murders. She also told about how the Family operated and the power that Charles Manson had over his followers. Kasabian said that no Family member ever refused an order from Manson.

The former Manson follower proved to be a very credible witness. She was unshaken by the cross-examination of the defense lawyers.

A Surprise From the President

The greatest setback to the prosecution's case was a slip of the tongue made by the president of the United States himself. On August 3, a headline in the *Los Angeles Times* said that President Nixon, who was following the progress of the case, had declared Charles Manson guilty at a conference of law-enforcement officials. Nixon had expressed his frustration with the media's glorification of Manson and expressed an opinion not meant for publication. Nixon later stated that he did not intend to speculate as to whether the Tate defendants were guilty or not. Nevertheless, the damage had been done. The headline in the paper said the president had declared Manson guilty—before his trial had ended. Kanarek immediately requested a mistrial. (A mistrial is declared when a case that has been compromised to a point where a jury cannot render a fair and unbiased verdict.)

Judge Older denied the motion "without prejudice," meaning that the defense could renew their request for a mistrial at a later date. The judge's reasoning was that since the jury was sequestered (locked away from television,

President Richard Nixon made a statement at a conference that led to the newspaper headline, "Manson Guilty, Nixon Declares!" Manson showed the headline to the jury, causing turmoil and halting the trial for a day.

newspapers, and any outside information sources that might influence their decision making) during the entire trial, they had not been exposed to President Nixon's statement. The trial would go on, much to the dismay of the lawyers for the defense.

The next day in court, Charles Manson suddenly produced a newspaper. On the front page was the headline, "Manson Guilty, Nixon Declares!"[7] Before anyone could stop him, Manson jumped up, held the newspaper over his head and exposed the headline to the eyes of the jury. Judge Older had Manson removed immediately. The proceedings were halted, and the jury members and alternates were questioned about what they had seen. Eleven had seen the full headline. Two had seen only the words "Manson Guilty." Four had seen only the newspaper or the name Manson. One had been looking at the clock on the court wall and so had seen nothing at all. After interviews, all eighteen jurors and alternates stated under oath that they had not been influenced in any way by the headline. It was discovered that defense attorney Daye Shinn had accidentally left the newspaper where Manson could lay his hands on it. Judge Older held Shinn in contempt and ordered him to spend three days in the county jail, commencing as soon as court adjourned.

Other Witnesses

After the testimony of star witness Linda Kasabian, the prosecution produced a number of other witnesses. One key witness was Juan Flynn, a ranch worker and cowboy who had spent much time at the Spahn Ranch. Flynn testified that after the Tate-LaBianca murders, he had an argument with Charles Manson. Flynn said that Manson grabbed him, put a knife to his throat, and shouted he was the one who was doing all of the killings. Manson then regained his self-control and put down the knife.

Manson's temper showed itself throughout the trial. On one occasion he jumped toward Judge Older and yelled, "Someone should cut your head off!"[8] Susan Atkins, Patricia Krenwinkel, and Leslie Van Houten leaped to their feet and started to chant loudly in Latin. The meaning of the words was not understandable. Once again, Manson and his followers were removed from the courtroom.

Other important witnesses to testify were Danny DeCarlo, Susan Atkins's former cell mates Virginia Graham and Ronnie Howard, and Manson Family member Paul Watkins. Watkins provided key testimony about the motives for the Tate-LaBianca killings. He explained Manson's Helter Skelter theory and plan in depth. Barbara Hoyt, who had recovered from her LSD-laced meal, also testified in support of Linda Kasabian's testimony.

Other bits of evidence strengthened the prosecution's case. Sergeant William Lee of the SID concluded that shell casings found at the Spahn Ranch during the raid had been fired by the same gun used to shoot victims at the Polanski house the night of the murder. The police had that murder weapon. They had the broken grips of that weapon, which were found at the murder site. It was shown that one of the pistol grips had blood on it that matched Jay Sebring's blood

Danny DeCarlo, who provided important evidence in the Manson trial, belonged to the Straight Satans motorcycle gang. Shown here are members of Hell's Angels, the most notorious biker gang of the 1960s.

type and subtype. There was also the evidence of the Buck knife, the nylon rope, Rosemary LaBianca's wallet, and the bloody clothes discovered by the TV news crew. Prosecutor Bugliosi also tied Manson's Helter Skelter theory and plan to the killings. In addition, Bugliosi showed that Manson had a prior connection to the Polanski home. On November 16, 1970, after twenty-two weeks of testimony, the prosecution rested its case.

The Defense

Judge Older told the lawyers defending Charles Manson and his female followers to call their first witness. Speaking for all the defense attorneys, Paul Fitzgerald stated, "Thank you, Your Honor. The defendants rest."[9]

The reply shocked the judge and almost everyone in the courtroom. It meant that the attorneys for the defense would not try to establish the innocence of their clients. The attorneys believed they had put up a strong defense during the cross-examination of the witnesses for the prosecution. They felt the prosecution had not established the guilt of their clients beyond a reasonable doubt. The defense was under no obligation to call witnesses. In fact, the defendants themselves were under no obligation to testify in their own behalf. Under the law, they could remain silent and allow the jury to judge the case based on the work of the prosecution.

However, that was not the end. Charles Manson had worked out a cunning scheme with Susan Atkins, Patricia Krenwinkel, and Leslie Van Houten. The women surprised their own lawyers by shouting to the judge that they wanted to testify. Manson's scheme was to have the women take all of the blame for the murders. They planned to state under oath that Manson had nothing to do with the crimes. It was their hope that Charles Manson would then be found not guilty and set free. Though their attorneys objected, the judge allowed the women to testify.

Ronald Hughes, who represented Leslie Van Houten, objected to allowing the women to testify. "I refuse to take part in any proceeding where I am forced to push a client out the window," said Hughes.[10] Hughes meant that he was not willing to sacrifice his client so Charles Manson could go free.

Susan Atkins, Patricia Krenwinkel, and Leslie Van Houten walk into court for their murder trial. Like other members of the Manson Family, each of the three women has scratched an X into her forehead in imitation of their leader.

Paul Fitzgerald, who represented Patricia Krenwinkel (and was the first lawyer to represent Manson, later resigning as a public defender to handle Krenwinkel's defense), tried to discourage his client from speaking on the stand. When Patricia Krenwinkel attempted to testify in court, Paul Fitzgerald refused to ask her any questions. Similarly, Daye Shinn refused to question Susan Atkins.

The following day, Charles Manson surprised everyone by stating that he too would now take the stand. He testified outside the presence of the jury. This was in case his testimony was incriminating to his codefendants. If it was, it would be identified and removed from the testimony presented to the jury. Charles Manson remained on the stand for one hour. One of his statements provides insight into how he felt about himself and society:

> I have ate out of your garbage cans to stay out of jail. I have wore your second-hand clothes . . . I have done my best to get along in your world and now you want to kill me . . . Ha! I'm already dead, have been all my life. I've spent twenty-three years in tombs that you built.[11]

After he was finished, Manson was asked if he then wanted to testify before the jury. He said that he did not. Judge Older then recessed the court for ten days to give lawyers time to prepare closing statements.

When court was again in session, the defense was minus one attorney. Ronald Hughes was not present. He had disappeared. Lawyer Maxwell Keith was named to replace Hughes. The prosecutor and defense attorney made their closing statements, and the case was turned over to the jury for deliberation.

chapter seven

THE SENTENCES AND THE AFTERMATH

TRIAL CONCLUDES—On January 15, 1971, some seven months after the start of the Tate-LaBianca murder trial, the jury began to deliberate. Security around the courthouse was very tight. A Manson follower had stolen a case of hand grenades from a California Marine base, and the Manson Family had issued threats that "Judgment Day"—the day the verdict was rendered—would be violent if the verdict was not favorable to the Manson Family.

The jury brought in a verdict on January 25, 1971. They found Charles Manson, Susan Atkins, Patricia Krenwinkel, and Leslie Van Houten guilty of first-degree murder. There was no violence—at that time.

There was one final act of bizarre behavior: Charles Manson shaved his head. Susan Atkins, Patricia Krenwinkel, and Leslie Van Houten shaved their heads, along with other female members of the Manson Family out on the street.

The penalty phase of the trial now began. It was

Manson, with his head recently shaved, is shown on the way to court to receive his sentence in the Tate-LaBianca murders.

the task of the jury to decide how the guilty parties should be punished. The prosecution argued for the death penalty. On March 29, 1971, the jury completed its deliberations. The four killers were handed down the most severe penalty of all: death. Judge Older ordered Manson to be delivered to the warden of the State Prison of the state of California at San Quentin. There he was to be put to death in the manner prescribed by the law of the State of California.

"You people have no authority over me," Manson shouted.

"You have judged yourselves," said Patricia Krenwinkel.

"The whole system is a game," stated Leslie Van Houten.

"Better lock your doors and watch your own kids," warned Susan Atkins.[1]

Charles Manson was taken to San Quentin to await execution. Krenwinkel, Van Houten, and Atkins were taken to a special wing at the California Institute for Women at Frontera until their sentences could be carried out. As in any case for which the defendants are sentenced to death, there were appeals to be filed, which would delay the sentences from being carried out.

Other Trials

Charles "Tex" Watson was eventually extradited from Texas. He stood trial separately for his part in the Tate-LaBianca murders. Prosecutor Vincent Bugliosi also won a conviction in that trial. Tex Watson was also sentenced to death.

Along with Bobby Beausoleil, Tex Watson, Charles Manson, and Susan Atkins were found guilty in the murder of Gary Hinman. Bruce Davis was convicted of the murders of Gary Hinman and Donald "Shorty" Shea, the ranch hand who had threatened to tell about the Family's illegal activities. Steven Grogan was also convicted of the murder of Shea. The convictions occurred even though the body of Donald "Shorty" Shea was not found until years later.

Defense attorney Ronald Hughes, who had disappeared after he opposed Manson and said he did not want Leslie Van Houten to testify, was found dead. His body was wedged between two boulders in the California desert. The authorities have never discovered the identity of his killer.

In 1972, the California Supreme Court declared the state's death penalty law unconstitutional. The death penalty would not be imposed on Manson, Watson, Atkins, Krenwinkel, Van Houten, or the others. The Manson Family members had their sentences commuted to life sentences.

More Violence

In 1975, a Manson Family member once again captured national news headlines. Lynette "Squeaky" Fromme made an attempt to take the life of U.S. President Gerald Ford. Fromme was armed and waiting as President Ford made his way through a crowd in Sacramento, California. She pulled out a hidden Colt .45 automatic pistol, aimed it at the president, and pulled the trigger. Luckily, the gun—which was fully loaded—did not go off. Fromme had not cocked it correctly. Secret Service men wrestled her to the ground and disarmed her. She was convicted of attempting to assassinate

Lynette "Squeaky" Fromme, a free member of the Manson Family, attempted to shoot President Gerald Ford in 1975. He was unhurt. Fromme was sentenced to life in prison.

President Gerald Ford and is currently serving a life sentence in the Federal Medical Facility at Carswell, Texas.

Where Are The Others?

Of the other members of the Manson Family who were convicted of murder, most are still incarcerated:

Bobby Beausoleil. Bobby Beausoleil married in 1982 while still serving a life sentence. He was transferred to a prison in Oregon in 1993 at his own request. His numerous requests for parole and appeals have been denied.

Bruce Davis. Bruce Davis is serving a life sentence at the California Men's Colony at San Luis Obispo, California. His twentieth request for parole was denied in July 2000.

Steve "Clem" Grogan. In 1979, Steve Grogan agreed to tell authorities the location of Donald "Shorty" Shea's body in exchange for a parole. A deal was made, and Grogan was freed.

Charles "Tex" Watson. Tex Watson is serving a life sentence at Mule Creek State Prison in Northern California. Watson no longer claims to do the devil's work. He has converted to Christianity and trained as a minister. He is married and has fathered four children while serving time in prison. His wife, Kristin, lives near the prison. Watson is a model prisoner but has been denied parole thirteen times. His last parole hearing was on October 20, 2001. His next hearing will be in 2005. Deborah Tate, the sister of the murdered Sharon Tate, has urged the parole board to keep Watson behind bars.

Susan Atkins. Susan Atkins is serving a life sentence at the California Institute for Women at Frontera. She has married twice while in prison. Atkins now expresses sorrow and regret over her crimes. She had been denied parole ten times. She will be eligible for parole again in 2006.

Patricia Krenwinkel. Patricia Krenwinkel is also at the California Institute for Women at Frontera serving a life sentence. She has expressed regret over her past crimes, but she did not attend her last parole hearing in 1997.

Leslie Van Houten. Leslie Van Houten is at the California Institute for Women at Frontera to serve a life sentence. In June 2002, she appeared before a parole board and pleaded for her freedom.

"One of the hardest things in dealing with having

Leslie Van Houten, shown in 2002. Van Houten has expressed remorse for her crimes, but all of her requests for parole have been denied.

contributed to murder is that there is no restitution; there is no making it right," Van Houten told the parole board.[2] It was Van Houten's fourteenth parole hearing. Her request for parole and freedom was denied.

Charles Manson. Charles Manson is currently being held in California Corcoran State Prison. He has received more mail than any other prisoner in United States prison system history.[3] Manson is kept isolated in his cell twenty-three hours a day. He is forbidden to interact with other inmates and is always handcuffed while being moved within the prison. Manson has been denied parole ten times. His last parole hearing was on April 24, 2002. His next parole hearing will be in the year 2007.

Charles Manson continued to have a great deal of notoriety worldwide. Over thirty British rock groups have played original songs written by Manson or songs written about him. Over forty European bands, especially ones in Germany, play and praise music by and for Charles Manson. The American rock group Guns 'N Roses has played Manson music.[4] There is even a Manson Appreciation Society known as Helter Skelter UK based in Warrington, Cheshire, England.

Conclusion

Over thirty years have passed since the Tate-LaBianca murders and the Charles Manson trial. Television shows still broadcast news about Manson and his Family members. In fact, much of the mail Charles Manson receives in prison is from young people who want to join his Family. There are

Charles Manson grins at the camera during a 1988 interview with Geraldo Rivera. One of the most notorious criminals in American history, Manson baffles and fascinates many people.

numerous Web sites devoted to Charles Manson, his Family, and their crimes.

In 1997, Charles Manson's parole hearing was video-taped and broadcast by Court TV. His parole was denied on the grounds that Manson "would pose an unreasonable risk and danger to society and a threat to public safety if released from prison."[5]

Manson calmly accepted the findings.

In June 2002, Leslie Van Houten had her fourteenth parole hearing. Van Houten has been a model prisoner since she began serving her sentence. In her thirty years in jail, she has earned two college degrees and assisted other inmates with educational programs. Her disciplinary record is clean. Some people think Van Houten and the other women have paid their debt to society. All of them, including Susan Atkins, now show deep remorse for their deeds.

However, Deputy District Attorney (LA) Steven Kay spoke at Van Houten's parole hearing and urged that she remain incarcerated.

"It can be determined that the gravity of the crime out-weighs her good behavior," Kay said. "She got her life. That's something the LaBiancas did not get. I think she should be grateful for that."[6]

Many people feel that Manson, Atkins, Van Houten and the others should never be released from prison. Perhaps they never will be. Who can say how much punishment is sufficient to atone for a spree of horrible murders?

Questions for Discussion

1. How did competition between different police divisions hinder the investigation of the Tate-LaBianca murders?

2. Do you think that immunity should ever be granted to individuals who participate in a conspiracy to commit murder? If so, in what circumstances?

3. Do you think that defendants who are not lawyers should be allowed to defend themselves in court?

4. In your opinion, should there have been a mistrial declared in the Tate-LaBianca trial after President Nixon stated that Charles Manson was guilty?

5. Do you think any of the defendants in the Tate-LaBianca murders should ever be paroled? Why or why not?

Chronology

November 12, 1934—Charles Manson is born in Cincinnati, Ohio.

1951—Manson commits his first federal crime at age sixteen. He drives a stolen car across state lines.

1967—Charles Manson is released from Terminal Island Reformatory in California. He goes to Haight-Ashbury in San Francisco and begins to recruit members of his cult family.

1968—The Manson Family, which includes Tex Watson, Susan Atkins, and Squeaky Fromme, takes up residence at the Spahn Movie Ranch and the Barker Ranch in the California desert.

July 25, 1969—Gary Hinman is attacked by members of the Manson Family at his beach cottage in Malibu, California.

July 31, 1969—Officers of the Los Angeles Sheriff's Office find Gary Hinman's dead body at his house.

August 6, 1969—Bobby Beausoleil is caught driving Gary Hinman's stolen car and is arrested.

August 8, 1969—Cult followers of Charles Manson murder Sharon Tate and her friends as part of Charles Manson's Helter Skelter scheme for global control.

August 9, 1969—A housekeeper discovers the victims at the murder scene and summons the Los Angeles Police Department. The murder investigation begins.

August 9, 1969 (night)—Leno and Rosemary LaBianca are murdered by members of the Manson Family.

August 10, 1969—The bodies of Leno and Rosemary LaBianca are discovered. Officers of the LAPD are alerted and arrive to investigate.

October 1969—Police raid the Barker Ranch to break up an auto-theft ring. Susan Atkins and Charles Manson are among those taken into custody.

November 1969—Susan Atkins brags about murders to her cell mates.

November 18, 1969—Deputy District Attorney Vincent Bugliosi is put in charge of the Tate-LaBianca case.

November 28, 1969—First trial of Bobby Beausoleil ends in a hung jury.

December 5, 1969—Susan Atkins testifies before the grand jury.

December 16–17, 1969—Atkins and Manson plead not guilty.

January–February 1970—Helter Skelter plot uncovered.

March 1970—Manson, Atkins, Van Houten, Krenwinkel, and Kasabian in court. Retrial of Bobby Beausoleil begins.

June 15, 1970—Tate-LaBianca murder trial officially begins.

July 27, 1970—Linda Kasabian, who made a deal with the prosecution, testifies.

August 3, 1970—Nixon declares Manson guilty.

November 16, 1970—The prosecution rests its case.

January 25, 1971—The jury finds Manson, Atkins, Krenwinkel, and Van Houten guilty.

March 29, 1971—Manson, Atkins, Krenwinkel, and Van Houten sentenced to death.

1972—The California Supreme Court declares the state's death penalty law unconstitutional.

Chapter Notes

Chapter 1. Bloody Messages

1. Deborah Fillmer, "Forensic Science & The Charles Manson Murders," n.d., *Manson Links*, <http://www.Cris.com/~dfillmer/manson.htm> (September 11, 2002).

2. Vincent Bugliosi with Curt Gentry, *Helter Skelter: The True Story of The Manson Murders* (New York: W.W. Norton & Co., 1974), p. 78.

3. Ibid., p. 163.

Chapter 2. The Cult and the Crimes

1. *Charles Manson: Bio/The Family/Sentencing*, n.d., <http://www.geocities.com/Tokyo/Temple/1510/cmanson.html> (September 11, 2002).

2. Marilyn Bardsley, "Charles Manson, the Manson Family—Confession," *The Crime Library*, n.d., <http://www.crimelibrary.com/serial_killers/notorious/manson/confess_4.html?sect=1> (September 11, 2002).

3. Richard Steele, "The Story of Squeaky," *Newsweek*, September 15, 1975, p. 18.

4. Tim Madison, "Astonishing Similarities Between Charles Manson & the Hindu God Shiva," 1997, <http://members.aol.com/KarolMay/manson.html> (September 11, 2002).

5. Ibid.

6. Doug Linder, *The Charles Manson (Tate–LaBianca Murder) Trial*, 2002, <http://www.law.umkc.edu/faculty/projects/ftrials/manson/mansonaccount.html> (January 22, 2004).

7. Vincent Bugliosi with Curt Gentry, *Helter Skelter:*

The True Story of The Manson Murders (New York: W.W. Norton & Co., 1974), p. 320.

8. Marilyn Bardsley, "Charles Manson: Murder!," *The Crime Library*, n.d., <http://www.crimelibrary.com/manson/mansonmain.htm> (September 11, 2002).

9. Bugliosi, p. 24.

Chapter 3. The Investigation

1. Vincent Bugliosi with Curt Gentry, *Helter Skelter: The True Story of The Manson Murders* (New York: W.W. Norton & Co., 1974), p. 26; see also Marilyn Bardsley, "Charles Manson: Murder!" *The Crime Library*, p. 2, n.d., <http://www.crimelibrary.com/serial_killers/notorious/manson/murder_1.html?sect=1> (September 11, 2002).

2. Marilyn Bardsley, "Charles Manson: Suspicion," *The Crime Library*, n.d., <http://www.crimelibrary.com/serial_killers/notorious/manson/suspicion_3.html?sect=1> (September 11, 2002).

3. Ibid.

4. Ibid.

Chapter 4. Breaks in the Case

1. Marilyn Bardsley, "Charles Manson: Confession," *The Crime Library*, n.d., <http://www.crimelibrary.com/serial_killers/notorious/manson/confess_4.html?sect=1> (September 11, 2002).

2. Ibid.

3. Vincent Bugliosi with Curt Gentry, *Helter Skelter: The True Story of The Manson Murders* (New York: W.W. Norton & Co., 1974), p. 125.

Chapter 5. The Prosecution Prepares

1. Vincent Bugliosi with Curt Gentry, *Helter Skelter: The True Story of The Manson Murders* (New York: W.W. Norton & Co., 1974), pp. 270–271.

2. Deborah Fillmer, "Forensic Science & The Charles

Manson Murders," n.d., *Manson Links*, <http://www.Cris.com/~dfillmer/manson.htm> (September 11, 2002).

3. Marilyn Bardsley, "Charles Manson: Prosecution," *The Crime Library*, n.d., <http://www.crimelibrary.com/manson/serial_killers/notorious/manson/prosecution_7.html?sect=1> (September 11, 2002).

Chapter 6. The Trial

1. Vincent Bugliosi with Curt Gentry, *Helter Skelter: The True Story of The Manson Murders* (New York: W.W. Norton & Co., 1974), p. 353.

2. Ibid., p. 395.

3. Marilyn Bardsley, "Charles Manson: Prosecution," *The Crime Library*, n.d., <http://www.crimelibrary.com/manson/serial_killers/notorious/manson/prosecution_7.html?sect=1> (September 11, 2002).

4. Doug Linder, *The Charles Manson (Tate–LaBianca Murder) Trial*, 2002, <http://www.law.umck.edu/faculty/projects/ftrials/manson/mansonaccount> (January 22, 2004).

5. Richard Steele, "The Story of Squeaky," *Newsweek*, September 15, 1975, p. 16.

6. Bugliosi, p. 421.

7. *Los Angeles Times*, August 3, 1970, p. 1.

8. Bardsley.

9. Bugliosi, p. 504.

10. Bardsley.

11. Linder.

Chapter 7. The Sentences and the Aftermath

1. Doug Linder, *The Charles Manson (Tate–LaBianca Murder) Trial*, 2002, <http://www.law.umck.edu/faculty/projects/ftrials/manson/mansonaccount> (January 22, 2004).

2. Linda Deutsch, "Former Manson Disciple Gets 14th Parole Denial," *The* (Bridgewater, N.J.) *Courier-News*, June 29, 2002, p. A7 .

3. Marilyn Bardsley, "Charles Manson: Where Are They Now?" *The Crime Library*, n.d., <http://www.crimelibrary.com/serial_killers/notorious/manson/now_9.html?sect=1> (September 11, 2002).

4. Marilyn Bardsley, "Charles Manson: Afterward," *The Crime Library*, n.d., <http://www.crimelibrary.com/serial_killers/notorious/manson/afterward_8.html?sect=> (September 11, 2002).

5. Marilyn Bardsley, "Charles Manson: Where Are They Now?"

6. Deutsch.

Glossary

accessory—One who is not present when a crime is committed but becomes guilty of that crime by instigating, commanding, or concealing the crime or by giving advice about it.

accomplice—One of several people involved in committing a crime.

acquit—To find a defendant not guilty of a crime.

affidavit—A sworn statement in writing.

arraign—To bring charges against a person in court.

bailiff—A sheriff or sheriff's officer or deputy.

confession—An acknowledgment of guilt.

conspiracy—A plan among a group of people to work together to commit a crime.

cross-examination—The questioning of a witness by the opposing attorney.

cult—A group of people fanatically devoted to a person, idea, or thing.

defendant—A person on trial for a crime.

district attorney—The prosecuting officer of a judicial district.

extradite—To return an accused person or fugitive from one nation or state to another.

grand jury—A group of citizens who meet to decide whether there is enough evidence to charge a particular person with a crime.

homicide—The killing of one person by another.

immunity—A legal condition granted to an individual making him or her safe from prosecution in a specific crime.

insanity defense—A "not guilty" plea based on the claim that the person did not know the difference between right and wrong or was not rational when the crime was committed.

mistrial—A trial that has no legal effect because of some error.

public defender—A lawyer appointed by the court to defend a person charged with a crime who cannot personally afford an attorney.

Further Reading

Burgan, Michael. *The Beatles*. Milwaukee, Wisc.: World Almanac Library, 2002.

Goodnough, David. *Cult Awareness: A Hot Issue*. Berkeley Heights, N.J.: Enslow Publishers, Inc., 2000.

Karson, Jill, ed. *Cults*. San Diego, Calif.: Greenhaven Press, 2000.

Steffens, Bradley, and Craig L. Staples. *The Trial of Charles Manson: California Cult Murders*. San Diego, Calif.: Lucent Books, 2002.

The Editors of Time-Life Books. *Turbulent Years: The 60s*. Alexandria, Va.: Time-Life Books, 1998.

Internet Addresses

An Account of the Charles Manson Trial
<http://www.law.umkc.edu/faculty/projects/ftrials/
manson/mansonaccount.html>

Charles Manson: The Crime Library
<http://www.crimelibrary.com/serial_killers/notorious/
manson/murder_1.html>

Index